SIMPLE TAROT CARD MEANINGS

Learn to Read Tarot Cards

Angie Green

TABLE OF CONTENTS

ABOUT THE SIMPLE TAROT

Hi, my name is Angie Green and like you, I struggled to learn the tarot card meanings and use tarot in my daily life for YEARS.

Learning how to read tarot doesn't have to be difficult. With a few simple tools and a little bit of parctice, you'll be reading tarot cards with confidence in no time.

When you know how to read tarot cards, you can use the tarot every single day to gain a deeper understanding of yourself, your problems, and the world around you. My goal is to help you get to a place where you can confidently read the tarot using your own deep knowledge of yourself and the cards.

I've created The Simple Tarot website and resources to make learning (and using) tarot cards simple and easy. This personal tarot journal is just one simple tool that will help you gain a deep understanding of yourself and your cards.

A companion journal, *The Simple Tarot Journal: A Personal Tarot Handbook*, is available if you would like to record your thoughts as you use this book.

For even more tarot resources, visit TheSimpleTarot.com for The Daily Tarot online, useful tarot spreads, a free printable tarot cheat sheet, and The Simple Tarot Deck.

HOW TO USE THIS BOOK

There is no right or wrong way to use this book. **There is only YOUR way.**

This book can be used with any Rider-Waite-Smith-based tarot deck and contains the 78 traditional tarot cards divided into the Major Arcana and Minor Arcana.

The Majors contain the first 22 cards (The Fool through The World) and each card represents a major archetype or life lesson.

The Minors describe everyday experiences, problems, and solutions. They are divided into four suits (Cups, Pentacles, Swords, and Wands). Each suit contains 10 numbered cards (Ace through Ten) plus four court cards (Page, Knight, Queen, and King).

Keywords, correspondences, descriptions, and samle readings are included for each card. This book is not meant to be memorized. It is a handy reference guide when you want to take your tarot understanding to a deeper level.

Each card can be interpreted in multiple ways. There is no right or wrong answer and you may intepret the cards differently. Be sure to record your own thoughts in the margins of this book or in the companion journal, *The Simple Tarot Journal: A Personal Tarot Handbook.*

The tarot cards shown are from The Simple Tarot Deck (Classic version without keywords).

This deck, as well as a Beginners version of the deck, with keywords printed right on the cards, is available from www.TheSimpleTarot.com.

THE FOOL

0 - The Fool

When you are wondering what will happen next, The Fool shows up to tell you something awesome (and totally unknown and unexpected) is about to happen. It's here to show you where you need to bring more fun, adventure, and playfulness into your life.

Traditionally, this card shows a young man blindly walking off the edge of a cliff, his face turned toward the sun. He's on his own private adventure and he doesn't have a clue about what's in front of him.

In one hand he carries a white rose (symbolizing his innocence) and the other hand holds a traveling hobo-bag (or man-purse-on-a-stick). His devoted little dog is following and they are striking out on an adventure.

The Fool is either the first or the last card of the Major Arcana, depending on how you choose to order your cards. It's given the number 0 (zero) and it both starts and completes the 22-card Hero's Journey through the major cards of the tarot.

The Fool is also known as "The Pioneer," "The Lunatic," and "The Foolish Man," which tells you a bit about the traditional meanings of this card.

In its most positive readings, The Fool is about starting a new adventure with enthusiasm and fresh hope. In a negative sense, it can be read as being stuck in immaturity, self-delusions, and short-term thinking.

Overall, The Fool is optimistic, self-focused, and blind to reality. But he's also got a cute dog and a nice purse, so you know everything will work out just fine!

KEYWORDS FOR THE FOOL TAROT CARD
Energetic adventures and a fresh start
Folly, mania, frenzy
Go for it - it's time to take a risk
Travel (in a literal sense) or a journey of self-discovery

KEYWORDS FOR THE FOOL REVERSED
Absence, thoughtlessness, carelessness
Apathy and being unprepared
Quit acting like a child - it's time to grow up

PATTERNS AND CORRESPONDENCES
Major Arcana = the cycle of your life's lessons and spiritual growth
Number 0 = beginnings and starting fresh
Zodiac sign = Aries, the start of the zodiac
Planet = Uranus, for novelty and unexpected events
Element = Air

THE FOOL READING FOR LOVE
The Fool is a pleasure-seeking, playful, and sociable card. If you are looking for love, it's a great card to inspire your romantic adventure. Create your online dating profile, take some big social risks, and put your beautiful self out into the world. Your "one true love" might not show up quickly, but at least you're going to have fun searching for them!

If you are questioning your current romance, The Fool can be read as a person inexperienced in love (either you or your partner), or it can be read about the state of your relationship in general.

Maybe you need to be more playful and bring the fun back into your partnership? Reconsider your romantic life as a crazy adventure and find new and exciting things to try together.

Rekindle the spark that brought you together by playing games, asking questions, and finding a hobby or physical activity you can share.

THE FOOL READING FOR WORK

If you are starting (or want to start) a new job, career path, or professional interest, The Fool supports you. Great things will come if you set aside your fear and your past mistakes, and move in this new direction.

It's time to take a risk with your work. Ask for the raise, take on a new project, or start studying something you know absolutely nothing about.

You will trip and make a fool of yourself. And that's wonderful! We only grow through experience, and The Fool is sending you on an adventure to gain the knowledge and confidence you need for this new life.

THE FOOL READING FOR HEALTH

If you are starting (or thinking about starting) a new health, nutrition, or exercise plan, The Fool is here for you! It's going to be a great adventure if you throw yourself into it. It's a fresh start, and you can put every health disappointment or failure behind you and begin again.

You may need more fun in your life. Even extreme introverts and natural hermits need to be connected to the greater world. All of your life's greatest lessons - and its most memorable events - will involve other people. The Fool can show you where to be more playful and social with others.

THE FOOL READING FOR MONEY AND FINANCES

The Fool is a risk-taking card. It's time to take a risk with your financial future and take a chance on a new adventure.

However, The Fool is also a crazy trickster and sometimes this card is a warning against being too foolish.

It's tough to have it both ways! The answer may not be logical or follow conventional wisdom, so you must follow your insight and intuition. Be careful and only risk the money you can afford to lose.

But spending on fun, adventures, and your social life may be what you need right now.

THE FOOL READING FOR SPIRITUAL GUIDANCE

If you are questioning your life's purpose, you are like The Fool at the beginning of a grand spiritual adventure. This is a quest of self-discovery, with ups and downs continuing through the other 21 cards of the Major Arcana.

It's a confusing time. You are so early in your journey that your destination is unknown and unseen. Right now, the path is unclear.

And that's exactly as it should be. If you can see 100% of the steps ahead of you, you are on the wrong path. This well-trod path created by someone else is not your journey. You are blazing a new trail, completely in line with your own dreams, values, and vision.

You only need to see the next step in front of you. Once you take the first step, continue moving forward and follow the threads pulling you. You'll eventually reach clarity and understanding, and your true destination will be revealed.

THE MAGICIAN

1 - The Magician

As The Fool begins his adventure through the tarot deck, The Magician is the first card he meets. This is why The Magician is numbered 1 (one), even though it's not the first card of the deck.

The Magician is in his garden, creating something magical. He is working with the four suits of the tarot (the cup, pentacle, sword, and wand) to draw creative energy from above, channeling it through himself to bring it into being in the physical world.

This is an active, outwardly-focused card. It is paired with The High Priestess card, which is The Magician's receptive and inwardly-focused magical counterpart.

The Magician is also known as "The Alchemist," the creator who makes something out of nothing. This card is about expressing your unique talents and turning them into something tangible in the world.

Although it seems a bit woo-woo, this is a very practical card. The Magician guides you to create an environment, triggers, and routines to regularly and consistently bring yourself to a state of creative flow where you can make your own magic.

KEYWORDS FOR THE MAGICIAN CARD

Empowered creativity

Self-confidence, the will, skill

Your talents, passions, and personal power

KEYWORDS FOR THE MAGICIAN REVERSED

You're not ready - don't take this risk

Scattered energy or resources, squandering your talents

Mental disease, disgrace

PATTERNS AND CORRESPONDENCES

Major Arcana = the basic lessons of life and personal growth

Number 1 = beginnings, creating something new

Zodiac sign = Aries, the start of the zodiac

Planet = Mercury, for cunning creativity

THE MAGICIAN READING FOR LOVE

The Magician can be a trickster in love, but this is a great card for lusty romances. It indicates a strong physical chemistry and the pure animal passion of attraction.

If you are looking to find or begin a new relationship, you will have to get out there and do the work. This is an active card. You are the one in control of your life and you are the only one capable of putting this goal into action.

If you are in a relationship, you can no longer ignore your problems as a couple. You need to actively communicate your needs and desires, and be honest about what is working and what isn't. Together, if you are both willing to do the work, you can come together to solve your problems.

THE MAGICIAN READING FOR WORK

When this card shows up, you are being told to use your natural skills and talents to shine. This is not the time to hide behind a mask, hold back your awesomeness, or promote someone else's agenda.

Your power and your passion are ready to be unleashed without limits. You've got this!

This is an active card, so set up the systems, routines, habits, and support you need to be your shiniest, boldest, and most creative self.

THE MAGICIAN READING FOR HEALTH

Are you at the beginnings of a quest for better health and fitness? You absolutely have the ability to accomplish your goals. This transformation is completely within your power.

What are your natural skills and talents? Strengthen your strengths and forget your weaknesses, at least for now. Throw all of your energy into the interests and activities where you have natural talents and passions. Double down on what you love.

If you are struggling with your health, seek out answers. Sitting around, passively waiting for things to change will not work. If you continue to ignore the problem, it will get worse so you must address it today.

THE MAGICIAN READING FOR MONEY AND FINANCES

Money, abundance, and wealth are all infinite. There is always more. You already have everything you need to get everything you desire.

It's time to manifest your visions into reality. Combine your unique talents with focused creativity to bring tangible things into the world. Money will come to you when you get extremely clear about pouring your you-ness into what you create and share. Don't copy or model your actions on anyone else. Create what only you can create.

It is your responsibility to share your unique talents and gifts with the world. You can't hide and expect to be successful. In return, the Universe will support and reward your creativity, integrity, and generosity.

THE MAGICIAN READING FOR SPIRITUAL GUIDANCE

Spirituality is the act of rising above yourself to feel a greater connection to the whole. When you are The Magician in your own life, you connect yourself to the Universe and all others within it.

Every single thing you are searching for is already within you. You already have everything you need to reach your biggest goals and dreams. While it may seem you are missing elements, they are only hidden.

You contain magic and this magic flows through you in every moment of every day. It is your job to actively channel this magic (or creativity or Source Energy or whatever you call it) from the Universe through your unique self and out into the world. The world needs more of what only you can create and give.

THE HIGH PRIESTESS

2 - The High Priestess

The High Priestess tarot card shows a beautiful woman sitting on a throne between two pillars, with a crescent moon crown and a giant crescent moon at her feet.

This card represents the inner wisdom deep within all of us. It is also known as "The Wise Woman" card. It is a receptive, inwardly-focused card with hints of mystery and deep secrets.

There is wisdom within each of us. Wisdom comes from our past mistakes, lessons, and experiences, but it also comes from deeper within us, encoded into our humanity by thousands of years of existence. The High Priestess card represents that deeper understanding.

When you see this card, something - possibly many things - remains hidden. There is a mystery here and it can only be uncovered by trusting your instincts and intuition.

This card is paired with The Magician, the active and outwardly-focused card that precedes it in the Major Arcana.

KEYWORDS FOR THE HIGH PRIESTESS TAROT CARD
Intuitive insight and wisdom
Secrets, mystery
Trust yourself and your instincts

KEYWORDS FOR THE HIGH PRIESTESS REVERSED
Blocked sight/insight/intuition
You've lost touch with yourself
Keep your secrets - don't share quite yet

PATTERNS AND CORRESPONDENCES
Major Arcana = the story of your life's lessons and spiritual growth
Zodiac signs = Pisces and Virgo
Planet = the Moon, which is only half seen and understood
Element = Water

THE HIGH PRIESTESS READING FOR LOVE
If you are single and looking for love, The High Priestess guides you to
go within yourself to find what you really desire. Are you looking for
a committed relationship with a true partner or some no-strings fun
with a handful of wonderful people? Or a mix of both? All answers are
perfectly okay, but only one of them is the right answer for you.

In a relationship, The High Priestess calls for you to trust your
"feminine" instincts. Be receptive to the love you are being given and
give open-hearted love in return.

In all relationships (not just romantic ones), keep the secrets you
are given and don't go blabbing or gossiping about somebody else's
business. Being a secret-keeper is an honor, so be worthy of that
responsibility by keeping your pretty mouth shut.

THE HIGH PRIESTESS READING FOR WORK
At work, things may not be what they seem. Something about this
situation remains hidden and it might not come to the surface for awhile
(if it ever does).

Even if you don't have all the information you need, you already know the answer. Go within yourself and let your intuition and instincts guide you. Control your ego and let yourself be open, receptive, and generous. Protect your work with strong boundaries, but let kindness lead.

If you are looking for a new career direction, spend time going deep within yourself to investigate your past, your patterns, and your secret desires. If money, age, experience, and fear weren't considerations, what would you really want to try?

THE HIGH PRIESTESS READING FOR HEALTH

This is the card of mysteries, secrets, and hidden information. If you are struggling with your health, get a full physical exam from head to toe, including blood tests and whatever else you need to get a true and complete picture of your health.

Good health isn't only about our physical bodies. Take care of your emotional and psychological health as well. Find a good therapist who can help you navigate the wilds of adulthood. Invest in becoming an expert on yourself.

THE HIGH PRIESTESS READING FOR MONEY

When it comes to financial decisions, something remains hidden from your understanding. Do not make rash decisions without fully understanding the consequences. Be careful of who you trust and always trust your own instincts.

This is not a time for big expenses or risky investments. Instead, build a solid foundation by creating an emergency fund, paying off debts, and insuring the things that are important to you. This may not sound sexy or exciting, but the security and comfort that comes when you no longer worry about money is the ultimate aphrodisiac.

THE HIGH PRIESTESS READING FOR SPIRITUALITY

The High Priestess is the deepest of your spiritual guides. She shows you the mysteries of your subconscious and helps you give a voice to your instincts.

Your subconscious speaks to you through your dreams. Keep a notebook by your bed and record your dreams immediately after waking up. Take note of any patterns or messages from your subconscious when you are dreaming and translate them into your daily life.

THE EMPRESS

3 - The Empress

The Empress tarot card shows a beautiful woman wearing a crown of twelve stars. She's lounging in her abundant garden. A waterfall flows from the background into a field of wheat in front of her.

The Empress stares boldly at you, welcoming you into her space. This is the card for fertility and abundance, and for the lusty Earth energy of sensual pleasures.

This card often shows up in tarot readings about family and fertility matters. The Empress strongly indicates fertility, pregnancy, and very positive partnership and parenting skills.

In addition, this is a great card for initiating creative projects.

The Empress is the "Earth Mother" who gives birth to all of your wishes and dreams. She represents all things motherly (from an ideal mother sense) and she is paired with the masculine father-figure of The Emperor. (NOTE: The Empress represents an ideal mother, not necessarily your mother).

The Empress tarot card symbolizes and represents the characteristics of sensuality, femininity, abundance and pleasure. However, when you see this card in a tarot reading it may indicate an actual woman in your life who plays the role of a maternal guide, domestic partner, or creative mentor.

KEYWORDS FOR THE EMPRESS TAROT CARD
Birthing abundance through creativity
Fertility, pregnancy
Marriage, good partnership and parenting skills
Abundant and sensual femininity

KEYWORDS FOR THE EMPRESS REVERSED
Creative block, barren ground
Stunted growth, not yet ready to change
Fertility or pregnancy issues or issues with your Mom

PATTERNS AND CORRESPONDENCES
Major Arcana = the teachers and lessons along your life's path
Number 3 = "and baby makes three"
Zodiac signs = Taurus and Libra
Planet = Venus for love, beauty, and sensual pleasures
Element = Earth

THE EMPRESS READING FOR LOVE
This is a very positive card for a long-term and traditional romantic relationship. If you desire a happy marriage, family, and/or babies - this is a great card for you.

But it's also a great card if you are looking for more of the sensual side of love. Bring out your playful sensuality and creativity to your love life. Learn how to take care of your own pleasure and practice enjoying the fun bits of intimate connection with a partner (or a few).

Be careful, though! This is an extremely positive card for fertility and pregnancy, so keep it wrapped if you don't want babies.

The Empress Reading for Work

The Empress births new projects in an abundant garden. But gardens take work. They don't happen on their own. Be prepared to plant the seeds, tend your garden, and work for the harvest.

She'll provide the abundant harvest, but only with your desire, dedication, work and direction. The work doesn't need to be drudgery (in fact, it shouldn't be!), but The Empress only works when you do.

This is a great card if you're looking to start or grow a creative project, either professionally or as a side hustle. The Empress LOVES creativity and artistic endeavors.

The Empress Reading for Health

Abundant health will be yours if you take the action to make it so. The Empress demands you put in the work before you can harvest the fruits of your labor.

So, yes, you'll have to eat well and in moderation, and you'll have to exercise in a way that pleases you. When you take care of yourself, The Empress will deliver.

If you're stuck, think of The Empress in her garden. Eat lots more vegetables at every meal and spend as much time as you can outside in a beautiful, natural place. You'll get to lounge like her after you've done the work of planting the seeds and maintaining them daily.

The Empress Reading for Money and Finances

When you want more money, resources, energy, time, or whatever you desire, The Empress will help you get it. But heed the advice above about work. You need to put in the effort before your efforts will be matched with abundance from The Empress.

You can't sit around waiting for things to happen. The Empress requires action, creativity, and initiative before she'll deliver.

But if you do the work aligned with your natural talents and passions in a way that benefits others, The Empress wants nothing more than your abundant success. She - and the Universe - will reward you financially and in all other ways.

THE EMPRESS READING FOR SPIRITUAL GUIDANCE

Spiritually, The Empress reminds you of the importance of the sensual pleasures of life. Yes, they're fleeting, but that's exactly why they need to be appreciated.

Don't sacrifice the enjoyments of connection and sensual delight in your quest to become enlightened and spiritually whole.

Our relationships can be our biggest challenges and teachers. Becoming vulnerable and intimate with others is an excellent way to understand your own desires, fears, and patterns. It also lets you practice the spiritual lessons you've learned. Create a supportive and loving circle of friends and grow together.

THE EMPEROR

4 - The Emperor

The Emperor is the "father figure" of the tarot cards, partnered with the motherly Empress. This card represents active, outwardly-focused energy of vision combined with discipline and perseverance.

Traditionally, this card shows an older man sitting on a throne carved with rams, staring boldly ahead. He sits more solidly than any of the King court cards and confronts your gaze directly. The Emperor won't back down.

He's the person you want in your reading, or in your life, when you are looking for practical, logical, and steady guidance. There's nothing wild here - it's all solid ambition, discipline, and honest hard work.

This card arrives when it's time to take hands-on, practical action toward your ambitious goals.

You MUST do the hard work required to see success. Half-measures won't do. You must commit to your dreams, with discipline, passion, and strategy.

Occasionally, this card indicates an actual person in your life who has the role of father figure, boss, or protector.

KEYWORDS FOR THE EMPEROR TAROT CARD
Action, discipline, strategy
A solid foundation from Doing The Work
To give (or command) respect
Reason, authority, will, ambition

KEYWORDS FOR THE EMPEROR REVERSED
Oppressive, shaky, or tyrannical leadership
Problems with ego, power, or maturity
Time to make a plan and do the work

PATTERNS AND CORRESPONDENCES
Major Arcana = the teachers and lessons along your life's path
Zodiac signs = Scorpio and Aries
Planet = Mars for ambition, victory, and the will
Element = Fire

THE EMPEROR READING FOR LOVE
This is a positive card for love, especially if you are looking for a relationship with a solid and stable person you can count on and respect at all times.

Build the strong foundations of all of your relationships through trust, commitment, and respect and you will be rewarded.

If you are having difficulties in your relationship, return to the basics of trust, love, and respect. Are you telling the truth? (You can't have trust without being trustworthy). Are you fully committed or do you have one foot out the door? Are you treating yourself with respect? Without the basics, your relationship will falter.

THE EMPEROR READING FOR WORK
The Emperor has one message for you and you must follow it. Do the work. Do the work. Do the work.

Be strategic in how you approach problems. Take the time to plan and build a strong base of daily actions.

This is a hands-on and practical card, but the focus is on creating the stability and security of a solid foundation.

Don't think of this as drudgery, though! The Emperor knows exactly what he wants and is passionately committed to accomplishing it, no matter how much fear, hard work, or idiotic problems stand in his way. This is his quest and he's fully committed to doing the work required.

THE EMPEROR READING FOR HEALTH

Again, this is a Do The Work card. If you want to see gains in your health or fitness, you can't wish for it or make plans. You must take action even when you don't want to. You can never give up.

Don't bother following the latest fad diet or buying a new fitness gadget. Your health will improve if you go back to implementing the basics.

Clean the junk out of your cupboards. Write down everything you eat. Walk more and sit less.

Don't search for better, simpler, or faster options. You already know what to do.

Now do it, every damn day. No excuses.

THE EMPEROR READING FOR MONEY AND FINANCES

You already know what to do, but now you actually need to do it.

Create a budget you can follow. Then follow it. Write down every penny as it enters or leaves your life.

Pay yourself first by having at least 5% of your income automatically withdrawn from your paycheck. Use the "Save More Tomorrow" system of 5% seems like too much right now.

Eliminate debt from your life. All of it. Even the "sensible" kind.

No, it's not sexy, but it sure is effective. The guidance from The Emperor isn't about fast, easy, or creative ways to make money. Bringing in more money isn't the solution. (Not yet anyway).

You're not ready for new money yet. First, you need to be responsible for what you already have. Until you can treat your current finances with respect, the Universe will see no reason to entrust you with more.

THE EMPEROR READING FOR SPIRITUAL GUIDANCE

Handling the practical and mundane activities of life (your work, your health, your money, etc.) are necessary before you can master the spiritual. If you don't take care of the boring-but-necessary basics, they will always be distractions that take you away from your higher purpose.

It's almost impossible to be your highest and best self when you are in pain, fearing the debt collectors, and hating your job. The Emperor understands this and wants you to take care of your practical, daily problems so you will have the strength and energy to move on to bigger things.

Master the mundane. Do the work - both the practical outer work and the necessary inner work of changing your mindset.

THE HIEROPHANT

5 - The Hierophant

The Hierophant tarot card represents conventional society, authority figures, and doing things the "right" way.

For people, especially the wild and unconventional rebels who follow the tarot's path, this pushes buttons.

Traditionally, The Hierophant card shows a man in a crown and robe with a scepter. He's not a king. It's clear he's a religious figure on a throne in front of two supplicants and with a set of crossed keys in between them.

The Hierophant is sometimes called "The Pope" card, which perfectly describes its role in the tarot. It's the card of ceremony, convention, and religion. This card honors tradition and established rules.

This card can represent a teacher of divine wisdom or it can carry a lesson about your role in society. The Hierophant also shows up when you are feeling the need for social approval and want to fit in.

Not all established rules and traditions are bad and sometimes it's better not to rock the boat. Especially when you're sitting in it!

It's natural to desire the acceptance and approval of the people you love. Being a member of a family, a community, and a society comes with certain (usually unstated) expectations and rules. This card represents those rules.

In a practical sense, this card could indicate a religious ceremony like a wedding or baptism.

KEYWORDS FOR THE HIEROPHANT TAROT CARD

Conventional wisdom
Society's expectations
Follow the traditional path
A religious ceremony, like a wedding or baptism

KEYWORDS FOR THE HIEROPHANT REVERSED

Nonconformist, rebel, outcast
Problems with society or authority
Question everything and be original

PATTERNS AND CORRESPONDENCES

Major Arcana = teachers and lessons along your life's journey
Zodiac sign = Taurus

THE HIEROPHANT READING FOR LOVE

Since this card indicates a traditional religious ceremony, it's a good indicator for a wedding. That doesn't mean a happy marriage, of course, but it's a start.

If you are looking for a traditional relationship, whatever that means for the society you live in, then this card is a positive sign.

If you are in or are looking for an unconventional relationship, things may get complicated. You or one (or all) of your partners may be worried about what other people will think or say about your choices. Be prepared for the fallout.

THE HIEROPHANT READING FOR WORK

The Hierophant shows up as a reminder of the common good. Although following the rules may feel like servitude or captivity, right now it's best to follow society's conventional path.

No matter how you feel about it, everyone has a need for social approval and is concerned with how they fit into their world.

Use The Hierophant to guide you toward a path you are comfortable with, within the system.

If you are looking for a mentor to guide you professionally, approach someone you look up to. Ask them for advice about a small and actionable problem in your life and then take their advice. Follow up to share your results and your sincere gratitude.

THE HIEROPHANT READING FOR HEALTH

If you've been struggling with your health or fitness, ask a wise teacher for help. A doctor, healer, or trainer may have solutions to the problems you are facing.

This means doing all of your annual checkups and following the boring-but-effective advice you know works.

The Hierophant leans toward conventional wisdom, so if you usually turn to alternative medicine or solutions, this is the time to get the opinion of someone more conventional. It's best to follow the established rules for now.

THE HIEROPHANT READING FOR MONEY AND FINANCES

Learn from other people's mistakes when it comes to managing your money and don't take risks on the unknown.

Read boring financial books with rich white dudes on the cover and follow their stodgy-but-effective advice. (Try Tony Robbins, Ray Dalio, and Warren Buffet to start).

It's best, at this time, to follow the established rules of money. Spend less than you earn, save for a rainy day, and make wise decisions with your resources.

Beware the need for social approval, however! Especially if it means trying to "keep up with the Jones."

The Jones are deeply in debt, miserably anxious when bills come, and are looking enviously at you!

Think long and hard about how you really feel about money. So much of our conditioning comes from societal beliefs we may not actually agree with. For example, if you believe the rich are all greedy and the poor are more generous and noble, where does your belief come from? How does it influence your actions?

And taking this further: Who benefits when you struggle with money or feel investing is too complicated? Who benefits when you (and people like you) stay poor, powerless, and without influence?

Our money and how we choose to earn it, spend it, save it, invest it, and give it away is one way we vote on what we want to exist in the world. Make your vote count by earning, spending, saving, investing, and giving as much as you can in ways aligned with your values.

THE HIEROPHANT READING FOR SPIRITUAL GUIDANCE

This card indicates the arrival or presence of a strong spiritual guide in your life, particularly if you're on a spiritual quest that includes religion in the traditional sense.

At the heart of every religious tradition is an understanding of unconditional love and how that love is always stronger than fear.

There is much to be learned from other religious and spiritual beliefs. This would be a good time to explore one (or more or all) of them deeply.

THE LOVERS

6 - The Lovers

Everyone loves The Lovers. This is the tarot card for true-love partnerships and long-term happy relationships.

In most traditional RW-based decks, The Lovers card shows a naked man and woman at the foot of the archangel Raphael, underneath a shining sun. (Raphael is the patron saint of healers, travelers, happy encounters, matchmakers, and the blind. Love is blind, after all).

You may be looking a new romance coming into your life, or you may be faced with making a choice between two very different situations. Either way, follow your heart.

This is sometimes called the "Romeo and Juliet" card, but that was a tragic and unhealthy relationship between children. Definitely NOT what this card is about!

Instead, think of this is as the "Gomez and Morticia" card, because they really had it going on. They show each other total respect, acceptance, and support and have a mad-passionate-freaky relationship, too.

But The Lovers is not a card about romantic love only. The Lovers represents a true, soul-level partnership where the personalities or elements are in total, healthy balance. This could be in a friendship, business partnership, or any place where two vibrant forces come together.

Along The Fool's journey through the Major Arcana, this is one of the first lessons: Two are stronger than one.

Keywords for The Lovers Tarot Card
A great love or business partnership
A choice between two options
Balancing of opposing forces
Attraction, beauty

Keywords for The Lovers Reversed
Differences, arguments
Divorce, a breakup
Take your time with this decision

Patterns and Correspondences
Major Arcana = the story of your life's journey and spiritual growth
Zodiac sign = Gemini, the twins

The Lovers Reading for Love
The Lovers tarot card is one of the best cards for a healthy soul-based love relationship. This could be a new love coming into your life or a deepening of an existing relationship. It's a wonderfully positive sign for beauty, attraction, affection, and long-lasting love.

If you're looking for a new relationship, you'll soon be falling in love, overcoming trials together, and coming closer as a partnership. It will be a long-lasting relationship based on respect and mutual admiration.

If you are looking for something casual, be aware that your emotions might become entangled. Be honest (with your partners and with yourself) about your desires and align your actions with your words. For many people, this means no sleep-overs or cuddling after the deed is done!

If you have to decide between two partners, choose the steadier option who will support you no matter what.

THE LOVERS READING FOR WORK
You may be faced with a choice between two opposing forces, people, roles, or positions. Something that looks good on paper might not be the right choice.

To make the best decision, follow your heart and make peace with your choice. It will be the right one for you, even if no one else understands.

This card may also indicate a positive business partnership entering your life. Is there someone in your professional world who balances your skills and weaknesses? Could you pair up to conquer your industry and projects together?

This will be an equal partnership, not a situation where you delegate tasks. Be sure you both understand your roles and get everything in writing before you commit to working together. This relationship will become long-lasting and mutually beneficial, but it will not last forever. Prepare now for the eventual end.

THE LOVERS READING FOR HEALTH
In this card, there is a balance of energy. When two people come together, they are stronger than one.

Use this balancing energy and the love of the people around you to guide you as you make decisions about your health.

Buddy up with a partner for accountability and treat your relationship with respect. Make a commitment to a health plan or routine (ideally with another person or larger community) and make that commitment the number one priority in your life.

You won't be any good to anyone if you are unhealthy, ill, or in pain. You must take care of yourself, but you don't have to go it alone. Ask for help and find a committed partner to support you as you make these life changes.

The Lovers Reading for Money and Finances

This is a positive card about partnership and the joining of two forces. You may be receiving money from a partnership, from a relationship, or from a choice you need to make.

It indicates a positive outcome. However, money and support may not come from the sources you expect.

If you need to choose between two options, don't convince yourself to choose the one that logically looks best on paper. Choose the one that feels best in your body. Focus on your long-term goals, not short-term gains.

The Lovers Reading for Spiritual Guidance

This card is about balance and the bringing together of two energies into one. Even though we must walk our inner spiritual journeys alone, the process will be easier and more enjoyable if you do it in step with soul-level friends.

Spiritual advancement doesn't happen in a vacuum. You need the support of the wise people around you to guide you as you move along this path.

Some of our greatest spiritual lessons come from interacting with the people in our lives. A key relationship may hold the wisdom, experience, and lessons you seek.

THE CHARIOT

7 - The Chariot

The Chariot vroom-vroom-vrooms into a tarot reading with a message of power through focused and deliberate action.

Traditionally, this card shows a man in a covered cart being pulled by a pair of Sphinxes. He wears a crown of stars and his armor is decorated with moons and astrological symbols.

The Chariot rides into the tarot right after the balanced partnership of The Lovers. When you have support, you're able to take action and tackle big challenges.

This lesson on The Fool's journey is about taking deliberate action now, even though you don't see the full path or even your destination.

You can't think, research, or plan your way to greater understanding. Taking action is the only way to learn more about yourself and your world.

It's time to move ahead. The way may not be crystal clear and you may not feel confident, but if you start with the first step, everything else falls into place. You will be able to adjust your course along the way.

Ultimately, you will experience victory. This is the time to move ahead with enthusiasm and commitment.

In a very literal interpretation, this card also indicates a journey or the purchase of an automobile.

KEYWORDS FOR THE CHARIOT TAROT CARD
Action and change
Move ahead with confidence
Triumph, success, victory
A vehicle or a journey

KEYWORDS FOR THE CHARIOT REVERSED
Losing your direction
Giving up the fight
Riot, arguments, litigation, defeat
Car or travel problems

PATTERNS AND CORRESPONDENCES
Major Arcana = the lessons along your life's journey
Zodiac sign = Cancer
Planet = Sagittarius

THE CHARIOT READING FOR LOVE
If you are looking for new love, you need to take the first step. Don't wait to see if your crush is interested or drop hints hoping they will make the first move. Just get their number and ask them out, like a grownup.

Ultimately, dating to find the right partner is a numbers game. Take deliberate and systematic action to meet and date as many people as you can, so you can find the person and the relationship you desire.

If you are in a relationship, ask for what you want. If your needs or desires are not getting met, be direct and ask for your partner to step up. Be kind, but don't hold back.

You can't control your partner's response or their actions, but you have full control over yours. If you're not getting what you want, the situation won't change unless you take the action to change it. It is your responsibility to step up and take care of yourself.

THE CHARIOT READING FOR WORK

Move ahead with your projects with bold confidence. You may not see the entire picture, but it will only clear up through action.

Procrastination and perfectionism are two ways we hold ourselves back out of fear and insecurity. If you are stalling on a project (or are 90% done and can't seem to get it completed), ask someone to hold you accountable for finishing it within a reasonable deadline.

If you are being pulled in many different directions, use your head to choose one and then take charge. This card is about action, not research, planning, or waiting. It's time to move forward with your big plans.

THE CHARIOT READING FOR HEALTH

Get moving. There's no simpler way to put it. If you're looking for guidance about your health, you must get off your butt and into some running shoes.

For success, you'll need to do the work. You can sit around feeling sorry for yourself, or wishing you had started a year ago, or feeling terrible about your situation.

Or you can take control of your life and do the work you know needs to be done. Become your own hero and inspiration and soon you'll be a hero and example for others.

THE CHARIOT READING FOR MONEY AND FINANCES

If you're looking to buy a car, this card indicates it is a good choice.

For everyone else, this is an action card. Take control of your financial situation by confronting your fears and ignorance. Buying lottery tickets doesn't count, either. This isn't about hopes and maybes. This card is about taking control and admitting to the reality of your current situation.

Think of your finances as a journey…Where does your journey end? (i.e. What's your goal?)

Where are you starting? (i.e. Get honest about your income, expenses, savings, and debt.)

Now, what's the first action step you need to take? Do it today. Don't put it off until tomorrow.

THE CHARIOT READING FOR SPIRITUAL GUIDANCE

This is a practical card, not a spiritual one. But every spiritual journeys requires action.

Are you meditating? Every day? Really every day? How about making it an every every day thing, not just a mostly every day thing?

What about reading spiritual books? Are you just reading them or are you doing the exercises and work of putting those lessons into practice in your own life?

Are you praying every day, if that's your thing? Do you have an altar in your house? Are you keeping a Gratitude Journal? Have you healed your relationships and forgiven everyone in your past (including yourself)?

What action steps can you take to deepen your connection to the spiritual world? Don't just think about them or write them down. Do them now.

STRENGTH

8 - Strength

In the RW-based tradition, the Strength tarot card shows a beautiful woman pressing the jaws of a lion closed. She has the infinity symbol over her head and she's wearing a belt of flowers.

This card, also known as "The Healer," takes the action-energy of The Chariot and adds in unconditional self-regard and centered confidence. Along The Fool's journey through the Major Arcana, this card represents the lessons you learn and the strength you gain when you understand and fully accept all aspects of yourself.

It's like you know, deep in your soul, that you have the inner strength to overcome any obstacle in your path.

Yeah, you'll be tested, but you don't even care. You've got this.

There might be lessons about trust and betrayal, friends and enemies, or the facade versus reality. But you have the courage and inner confidence to survive and thrive through them all.

In some tarot decks, this card is given the number 11 (eleven) instead of 8 (eight), swapping places with the Justice card.

KEYWORDS FOR THE STRENGTH TAROT CARD

Inner strength

Power, energy, courage, action

Unconditional acceptance of yourself

Take control of your life

KEYWORDS FOR THE STRENGTH CARD REVERSED

Abuse of power

Letting fear rule

Discord, disgrace

Things are out of your control

PATTERNS AND CORRESPONDENCES

Major Arcana = the lessons of your life's path

Zodiac sign = Leo, the lion

STRENGTH READING FOR LOVE

The Strength card is a bit more about pure animalistic lust than it is about love. Which, if that's what you're after, is a very fun thing.

If you are looking for a new relationship, be sure you are getting what you want. If you want a bit of fun, Strength shows up to point toward ways you can satisfy your desires.

If you're looking for something serious, Strength shows up as a warning: you need to control your animal instincts and look for a deeper partnership. Don't let chemistry (or the lack of it) rule your decisions. Look for the partners who make you feel good, happy, loving, and strong.

Love is the key to being fearless and brave. Loving and being loved are a strong foundation for courage.

When the Strength card arrives in a reading, it indicates you will be tested, but the unconditional love you feel (toward yourself and others) can help guide your way. And if you're feeling lusty, go for it!

Strength Reading for Work

You already have everything you need to overcome the obstacles in front of you. You have the power, energy, courage, and creativity to succeed. Now you need to take action and get to work!

If coworkers, clients, or other people in your professional world are giving you trouble, you need to take control. Set the rules and make sure everyone knows where you stand.

You hold the reins here. There may be tests along the way, but you will be successful.

If you are feeling uncertain about your future professional path, spend time assessing your personal strengths and weaknesses. Identify your natural talents and gifts, as well as the skills you've learned over time. Once you become intimately familiar with your unique abilities and interests, you can create a path perfect for you.

Strength Reading for Health

The Strength card is a positive tarot card for abundant good health. It's known as "the Healer," after all.

You have the power to master your vices and the habits that are damaging your health. While you may not be able to control everything, you are in control when it comes to your thoughts, your choices, and your actions.

Be exceptionally kind to yourself and show yourself the unconditional love you deserve. When you "treat yourself," treat yourself well. Don't use sugar, alcohol, or avoidance activities. Make choices that give you even more power, more energy, and more life.

And if you are struggling with positive self-regard, ask for help from a professional. Sometimes we all need an outside perspective to show us where we are being held back by our own blindness and limiting beliefs.

STRENGTH READING FOR MONEY AND FINANCES

Keep to your plans and don't lose hope. Things may not be going as well as you'd like, but you absolutely have the power and ability to control what matters.

You may not be able to control the stock market, or when you get paid, or even if you get paid at all. But you can control your thoughts, words, choices, and actions. And you have a lot of power there.

Ask yourself: Are you treating money with respect? Are you treating your money with respect? If you treated your best friend the way you treat money, would they want to hang out with you? If you treated your boss the way you treat money, would they give you more responsibility and trust?

The Universe wants you to be rich. It's the only way you'll be able to accomplish your biggest and most generous goals and dreams.

Being poor doesn't serve anyone. (Who is actually served when you and people like you are poor? Who benefits when you are struggling and without influence or power?)

So, do you want to be rich or poor? And what are you going to do about it?

STRENGTH READING FOR SPIRITUAL GUIDANCE

The spiritual lessons of the Strength card come from mastering yourself with acceptance and unconditional love.

On a daily basis, do you treat yourself as well as you treat the people/ deities/energies/whatever you worship?

Do you think these people/deities/energies want you to suffer? Or do they want you to shine? Who knows more, you or them?

If you are a believer, this is the ultimate WWJD question: Do you treat yourself with the unconditional love Jesus shows you?

THE HERMIT

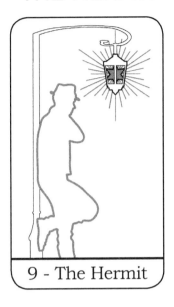

9 - The Hermit

The Hermit tarot card is the card of solitude and withdrawal.

Traditionally, this card shows an old man holding a staff in one hand and a lit lantern in the other. It's a quiet and simple card with a powerful message.

When you are faced with a tough situation or difficult decision, The Hermit whispers, "You already have all of the answers you need. You just need to go deep within yourself to find them."

Along The Fool's journey through the Major Arcana, this is the lesson of trusting yourself. Maturity comes when you feel confident in your own voice. But before you gain that confidence and maturity, you must first learn what your voice has to say.

Hone your intuition through deep self-knowledge. Quiet contemplation, meditation, and removal from the stresses and hassles of your daily life will help you strengthen your intuition. When you go within yourself, you will find the solutions you are looking for.

Keywords for The Hermit Tarot Card

Spiritual illumination
Go within for your answers
Eliminate the "busyness" to open yourself to growth
Remove yourself from this situation

Keywords for The Hermit Reversed

Repeating your past mistakes
Resisting your inner voice
Concealment, disguise
Isolation, loneliness, too much solitude

Patterns and Correspondences of The Hermit Card

Major Arcana = the lessons and journey of your spiritual growth
Zodiac sign = Virgo

The Hermit Reading for Love

The Hermit is a very solitary card. When this card arrives during a reading about love, it usually indicates you are not yet ready for the relationship you are seeking.

Are you too tied to the past? Are you wishy-washy about your desires? Do you know the type of relationship you want? The only way to know is to go within and trust the answers you find there.

If you are in a relationship, be honest with yourself. If you are spending too much time focused on the other person, you may not be getting your own needs met. Do you know what you really want?

If possible, remove yourself from your social commitments for a few days or weeks. Use your free time to think, journal, and explore what you desire and fear.

The Hermit Reading for Work

If you are struggling with a project for work, you will find the answers through removing yourself from the situation (as much as you can).

Give yourself some space and time away from the problem. Clear the decks and don't let yourself get seduced by constant busyness. Trust yourself to find a different way.

The quiet contemplation of this problem will bring clarity. You may be so enmeshed in the problem you don't see it clearly. If you step back, you will better be able to see all sides and come up with creative ways to deal with the issue.

THE HERMIT READING FOR HEALTH

The Hermit card is a meditative and restive card. If you are looking for ways to increase your fitness, try yoga, tai chi or long walks alone.

Rest, relaxation, and especially sleep are vital to your health. Reduce the stress in your life, say a strong NO to obligations and busyness, and take care of yourself. Put your own needs first.

It's very common to use "busyness" as a way of avoiding our problems. Keeping ourselves "too busy" means we never have to deal with the fear, pain, and suck of life.

The Hermit requires a different way. When you eliminate all of the busyness and sit with the problem, you will eventually find a new way of dealing with it. Yes, it's uncomfortable, but the only way out is through.

THE HERMIT READING FOR MONEY AND FINANCES

Financially, you need to conserve your resources. This is not the time for extravagant purchases or risky investments.

However, if you are considering investing in yourself through education or professional development, it may be a good use of your money.

If you are looking for additional income, tap into your existing talents and experience. Go within for your answers. They are already there.

And if you have repeated the same problems with money throughout your life, deal with them by finding their root cause. Dive deep into your beliefs about money, rich people, and poverty. Create a mindset of abundance in all things and give fear and judgments the boot.

The Hermit Reading for Spiritual Guidance

The Hermit goes deep into the woods or to the top of the mountain to be alone with his thoughts. You don't need to go that far. You can do it from anywhere.

Meditation is one of the keys to clarity and inner peace. It doesn't have to be 20 minutes with your legs crossed on a pillow, ohmming for world peace.

Meditation can be as simple as long walks alone, focusing your thoughts on an idea or question. It could be pacing through a labyrinth. Or coloring in a coloring book like a kid. For me, it's being led across the dance floor, breath-to-breath with my tango partner.

The Hermit is a reminder that everything you need is already within you. If you're willing to look inside yourself and accept everything you find there, you'll find the spiritual guidance you seek.

This is a simple lesson and one that will repeat throughout your life. But simple doesn't mean easy, which is why this lesson will repeat itself again and again until you fully integrate it into practice.

THE WHEEL OF FORTUNE

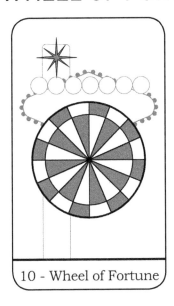

10 - Wheel of Fortune

Usually a good omen, The Wheel of Fortune tarot card suggests lucky success and good fortune. There is an element of things changing for the better, so go for it and take your chances. Good luck is usually about being well prepared and standing in the right place at the right time.

Of course, not all luck is good, so the meaning of this card does depend on the other cards surrounding it. Regardless, if you get The Wheel of Fortune in a tarot card reading, your luck is about to change.

This card is sometimes called "the Gambler," because it deals with luck, fate, and other things outside your control.

In The Fool's journey through the Major Arcana, this card's lessons are about control. No matter how much you prepare or how hard you work, you can't always control the outcome. Sometimes you get lucky and sometimes luck is not on your side.

KEYWORDS FOR THE WHEEL OF FORTUNE TAROT CARD

Success, good luck
A turning point - go for it!
Your luck is about to change
Gambling

KEYWORDS FOR THE WHEEL OF FORTUNE REVERSED

Bad luck, a downturn
Return to your values
Negative external forces

PATTERNS AND CORRESPONDENCES

Major Arcana = the story of your life's journey and spiritual growth
Zodiac sign = Scorpio, Aquarius, Leo, and Taurus, the fixed signs of the zodiac
Planet = Jupiter

THE WHEEL OF FORTUNE READING FOR LOVE

Lucky in love! If you are looking for a new relationship, you need to put yourself out there. Your perfect partner isn't going to arrive on your doorstep wrapped in a bow, so leave the house every day looking and feeling your best.

Like gambling, dating is a numbers game. You'll need to meet and kiss a lot of frogs before you find the perfect match, so do everything within your power to increase your odds of success.

If you are in an existing relationship, a major change is in the works. The factors are favorable, so go forward with bravery and honesty. Ask for what you want. There's a very good chance you'll get it, or something even better!

THE WHEEL OF FORTUNE READING FOR WORK

This is a great card if you are looking for a raise or a promotion. Take your chances and ask for both.

There will soon be a major change in your life. This card works quickly. To help your luck along, put yourself out there by asking inspiring and influential people for actionable advice about a single problem you are facing. Take their advice and follow up with them with your results. You'll be making your own luck in no time!

THE WHEEL OF FORTUNE READING FOR HEALTH
All signs point toward GO when it comes to your health and fitness.

Now is a great time to sign up for a 5K or commit to doing Whole30 for a month. You can totally do it and the Universe will conspire to help make your desires come true.

The Wheel of Fortune can sometimes indicate an out-of-control gambling habit. If your hobby is fueled by adrenaline and you've tried to quit, share your situation with someone you trust. You will be lucky again, but only when you approach your desires from a place of humility, vulnerability, and open-hearted honesty.

THE WHEEL OF FORTUNE READING FOR MONEY AND FINANCES
This is the card of "the Gambler," so be smart and don't gamble any money you can't risk losing forever.

If you want to play the lottery, have fun with it and do it for entertainment. No matter how lucky The Wheel of Fortune seems, it doesn't offset the horrendous odds of actually winning the jackpot.

But, life is random and stranger things have happened. Your luck is about to change and it appears good fortune is on its way.

Help your luck along by being prepared. Stock up your resources and make yourself available for last-minute awesome deals, opportunities, and chances. Don't tie up your money in expensive toys.

Investigate all opportunities thoroughly. Reduce and mitigate your risks. All of your gains will be made when you buy, not when you sell, so buy when the market value is at its lowest point.

When you don't need the money, gambling and taking risks becomes a fun game.

THE WHEEL OF FORTUNE READING FOR SPIRITUAL GUIDANCE

Luck, destiny, fate - whatever you call them, they come from somewhere. Where do you think that is?

We all make our own luck through our focused beliefs and desires. It's possible to make yourself into an abundantly lucky person through a positive, loving mindset and compassionate, decisive action. When you have more than enough good fortune (and luck), you can share your excess abundance with the world.

JUSTICE

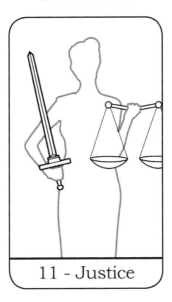

11 - Justice

If you've been naughty, the Justice card is a bitch. This tarot card arrives when things are out of balance and it highlights the consequences of your behavior.

In The Fool's journey through the Major Arcana, Justice represents the lesson of the ultimate natural law - the law of cause and effect.

If things seem out of whack, the Justice card has one message for you: the Universe is playing fair. You may not like the outcome, but it will be based on harmony and fairness for the greater good.

Traditionally, the Justice card shows a serious-looking woman seated on a throne holding a sword upright in one hand and a set of scales in balance in the other.

This card carries an obvious message about judgment and fairness. As a judge, the Justice card carries the heavy weight of representing the consequences of one's actions.

In a literal sense, this card anticipates a legal situation or judgment.

In some tarot decks, this card is switched with the Strength card and given the number of 8 (eight), placing it between The Chariot and The Hermit in the Major Arcana.

Keywords for the Justice Tarot Card
Fairness, balanced judgment
The consequences of one's behavior
Seek win-win situations
Do the right thing

Keywords for the Justice Card Reversed
Legal complications
Bigotry, unfairness
Dishonesty, lack of accountability
Get back into balance

Patterns and Correspondences
Major Arcana = the lessons and teachers along your life's journey
Zodiac sign = Libra

Justice Reading for Love
This is not a great card for finding new love, unfortunately. The Justice card can indicate purity and virginity, neither of which help any intimate romantic relationship.

But if you are going through tough times in your relationship, the Justice card can be a good sign. It reminds you to fight fair and to balance your needs with the needs of your partner.

Look at the situation from your partner's side and try to come up with a compromise you both feel happy about. There are always win-win solutions to your problems, so work together to find an answer that suits you both.

If one of you has been dishonest or wishy-washy, the truth will come out. This is not a negative card, though, so don't expect disaster. One of you could have deeper feelings than anticipated and that truth would be revealed as well. Anything unfair, manipulative, or unbalanced will become apparent.

JUSTICE READING FOR WORK

Do not cut corners, take shortcuts, or try to be sneaky. The only way to win is by playing fair and doing the right thing.

When it comes to making decisions, think of the long-term results. Take your time to weigh the consequences of each path and use balanced judgment to make the right decision for everyone involved.

The consequences of your past bad behaviors may be coming to light. It's always better to own up to them, apologize, and come up with a plan for reparations instead of trying to hide your mistakes away.

Don't let your ego get in the way of your integrity. Do the right thing with grace and forgiveness.

JUSTICE READING FOR HEALTH

There is balance in everything, so balance your behaviors when it comes to your health and fitness.

It is just as bad to go overboard with a new health regime or diet as it is to sit on the couch eating an entire box of Cheez-its.

Payment is due today for yesterday's bad behavior. Don't make the future worse by continuing your actions or ignoring the signs you need to change.

Think of the law of cause and effect, and change your behavior accordingly.

JUSTICE READING FOR MONEY AND FINANCES

Money loves clarity and the Justice card can help you provide it. Telling the truth about your financial situation (every last embarrassing detail) will allow you to change it.

It's the basic law of cause-and-effect in action. If you treat money with respect and fairness, it will treat you the same.

Take a careful look at your finances without judgment or shame. They are just numbers. They don't represent your worth.

Pretend you are an impartial outsider as you look at these numbers. What advice would you give yourself, if you weren't so emotionally invested in the situation?

How you earn, spend, save, and invest your money represents what you value in the world. It's one way of voting on what you'd like to exist.

Align your financial decisions, even little ones like where you choose to buy lunch, with your values and integrity. Your money is power, so use it wisely.

JUSTICE READING FOR SPIRITUAL GUIDANCE

Spirituality means different things for different people, but at the heart of any spiritual quest is a search for meaning. We are looking for our place and our purpose in the world.

The Justice card reminds you to use clear-headed thinking to judge your own behavior and choices, in large and small matters in your daily life.

There is a higher truth to the mundane decisions that rule our lives. When our daily actions are in line with our values, we are living in integrity.

We create our own place and purpose through these daily actions. When our actions are in alignment with our values and are connected to others, we are living a spiritual life.

THE HANGED MAN

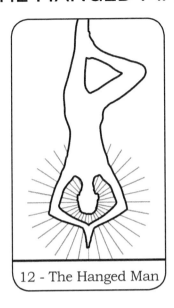

12 - The Hanged Man

The Hanged Man tarot card shows a man dangling upside-down from one ankle. A light, almost like a halo, radiates behind his head. Despite his uncomfortable position, he appears to be at peace with his situation.

There is nothing struggling or sad about this card. In fact, The Hanged Man is very serene and accepting of this fate.

Along The Fool's journey through the Major Arcana, this card represents the lessons learned when you take responsibility for your actions and then accept their consequences with grace. It represents the ultimate in letting go of what you can't control.

You need to release the tight grip you hold on your ideas and the situation at hand. That won't work anymore, so become the agent of change by making a sacrifice (i.e. by being the "better man") to break the old patterns.

When you feel betrayed, like a victim, or ashamed of your own actions, look at things from a different point of view. You need a change of perspective.

This card represents the first phrase of the Serenity Prayer, "Please grant me the serenity to accept the things I cannot change…" We can only control ourselves. Everything else we must release and accept with grace.

Keywords for The Hanged Man Tarot Card
Sacrifice for the greater good
Release and let go
Look at things differently
Wisdom, trials, intuition

Keywords for The Hanged Man Reversed
It's over and there's no going back
Selfishness
Feeling like a victim
Being framed, betrayal

Patterns and Correspondence
Major Arcana = the lessons along your journey toward spiritual growth
Zodiac sign = Pisces
Planet = Neptune
Element = Water

The Hanged Man Reading for Love
If you are looking for love, The Hanged Man wants you to do something different. Change your hairstyle, try a new hobby, and change your online dating tactics. Whatever you've been doing, try the opposite.

You don't need to change yourself, but you do need to change your patterns. What you've been doing so far hasn't resulted in the relationship you want, so you must try something radically different.

If you are in a relationship with problems, put aside your own desires and focus on finding a solution that is best for the both of you. When you release your pain and let go of your resentments, you'll be able to follow a new path to brings you closer together.

If your heart is hurting, The Hanged Man is advising to you release the past and let go. If you were meant to be together, it would have happened. You need to trust everything is working out exactly as it should be. There is someone wonderful waiting for you as soon as you move on from your heartbreak.

In all cases, you must accept the situation as it is, not as you wish it would be. It is painful when reality doesn't match our desires, but the only way to move forward is to accept that much of the world is out of our control. With acceptance comes peace and clarity.

THE HANGED MAN READING FOR WORK

If you are having challenges at work, use your inner wisdom and intuition to sort through the situation. Take your time and look at things from a different perspective.

This would be a great time to put the career of someone else before your own. Mentor a rising star, sing the praises of someone deserving, or do some pro-bono work to help a cause you believe in.

Striving hard all the time will get you moving fast, but you may be moving in the wrong direction.

When you take action without first getting clear on your true goals and values, your energy will be scattered. Pull back and refocus on the essential.

The Hanged Man will guide you to understand the difference between "important" and "urgent." Focus your time and energy on being effective, not just efficient.

THE HANGED MAN READING FOR HEALTH

Relieve the pressure from yourself and look at your health and fitness from a different point of view. If you've been doing lots of yoga, maybe it's time to add in running or kickboxing to your routine. Or vice versa.

You can't control everything about your health, of course, but The Hanged Man is here to advise you on what you can control. Release the rest and don't worry about things you can't influence.

Take full responsibility for what you can control (your thoughts, beliefs, words, choices, and actions) and let everything else go. If it's outside of your control, it's not your concern.

The Hanged Man Reading for Money

Taking care of your money can be boring. Annuities, insurance plans, and mutual funds are the parts of adult life that are necessary, but not sexy.

Understanding the basics of money is your responsibility. It's time to look at your financial situation differently.

If you've been frugal and miserly, finally go on your dream vacation. If you normally treat others to dinner or drinks, let someone else pick up the tab. And if you are using your credit cards, imagine what it would feel like to have no debt at all.

Flip your attitude about your finances. When you are in control of your money, you have power over what you want to exist in your world.

Look at your financial choices through the lens of your values and make your choices from a place of power and abundance.

The Hanged Man Reading for Spiritual Guidance

This is a great card to help you focus your spiritual intuition. When you look deep within yourself, you'll find the peace you're searching for.

Everyone feels shame and embarrassment about their past (and often current) actions, choices, and situation. Everyone.

The Hanged Man is your spiritual reminder that the only path to enlightenment involves fully accepting the awful bits about ourselves. Only then can we move forward with unconditional self-love.

You don't need to be selfless or a martyr to be spiritual. You just need to be fully yourself.

DEATH

13 - Death

The Death tarot card scares people. It's the card that elicits the most gasps and cringes when it comes up in a reading.

But the Death card is one of the most misunderstood cards in the deck. Traditionally, this card shows a skeleton on top of a horse, wearing armor and holding a flag. A religious man is appealing to Death and the dead and sick lay on the ground in front of him.

Despite the imagery, this card rarely has anything to do with actual, physical death. Instead, it's a card of rebirth. It's about change and letting go of the past to move on to something better.

Like the mythical Phoenix rising from the ashes, the Death card indicates one cycle is ending and another is beginning. There is a major transition happening where you must leave your old life and start something new.

In The Fool's journey through the Major Arcana, this card follows the sacrifice and acceptance of The Hanged Man and represents what happens after that sacrifice. Once you let go of what you can't control, you will be reborn into a place of clarity, acceptance, and action.

KEYWORDS FOR THE DEATH TAROT CARD

Transformative rebirth, like the Phoenix
Final endings, involuntary change
The end of one cycle and beginning of the next
Letting go and moving on

KEYWORDS FOR THE DEATH CARD REVERSED

Lethargy, sleep, inertia
Refusal to accept change
Stagnation
Hope destroyed

PATTERNS AND CORRESPONDENCES

Major Arcana = the lessons along your life's journey
Number 13 = an "unlucky" number, as in Friday the 13th
Zodiac sign = Scorpio

THE DEATH READING FOR LOVE

If you're looking for new love, you must be absolutely, completely, and totally over the relationships you've had in the past.

You must move on. Your next relationship will be radically different from anything you've experienced before, so quit carrying old baggage. It's too burdensome and you won't need it anymore. You must transform your beliefs, habits, and patterns to allow something new to enter your life.

The Death card is a card of final endings, so if you are worried about the state of your current relationship, this doesn't bode well.

You must give up the past, which includes your dreams, expectations, and ideas of what the "perfect" relationship looks like, before you can find the love you're meant to have.

THE DEATH READING FOR WORK

The Death card indicates involuntary changes and major transformations. Be prepared for the worst, but expect the best eventual outcome.

This is actually a positive card, so even if things are dire (you get fired, or lose the promotion, or screw up somehow), it really is for the best. Things will work out, although probably not the way you want or expect.

Let go of what isn't serving you and your dreams, and allow for new growth in your life. You must let this situation end completely before you will be able to move on to something better.

THE DEATH READING FOR HEALTH
Does the Death card sometimes indicate physical death? Yes, sometimes. Rarely. Almost never. It's not even worth worrying about.

Because people die. It's what we do. We don't like to think about it, talk about it, or even acknowledge it. But it is one of the few guarantees in life.

What really matters, though, is how you live, and that's the ultimate message of the Death card.

You get a second chance with every new minute of every day. Don't burden yourself with the baggage of your past. Start fresh by putting all of your past where it belongs - behind you. Use this time in your life for regeneration and rebirth.

Let go of what doesn't serve you, such as guilt, body shame, and Doritos. Focus instead on your transformation. You are the alchemist of your life and the only one in control of the outcome.

THE DEATH READING FOR MONEY AND FINANCES
There is a big change coming. BIG. And you're probably not prepared for it.

Instead of taking a big risk right now, put your financial foundation in order. Are you debt-free with enough savings to live off of for the next 6 months? Work toward that goal, not some pie-in-the-sky possibility. With that kind of financial security underneath you, you'll be able to handle almost everything thrown your way, including once-in-a-lifetime opportunities and investments.

If you've made big financial mistakes in the past, move on with acceptance and integrity. You can transform your relationship with money by taking control today.

THE DEATH READING FOR SPIRITUAL GUIDANCE

You must give up the past and your guilt, shame, and regrets, before you can move on. Fully embrace yourself - all the good and all the bad - to allow room for new spiritual growth.

Spiritually, we are all seeking wholeness and belonging. We want to find our place in the world.

The Death tarot card isn't the end of the world. It's our wake-up call to fully embrace the present moment and the few things fully within our control.

TEMPERANCE

14 - Temperance

The Temperance tarot card seems boring, especially sandwiched between the Death card and The Devil. But Temperance is about boring, gentle, and wonderful things, specifically the peace and comfort that surrounds you when your life is in balance.

Traditionally, the Temperance card shows the archangel Michael pouring liquid from one cup to another. One of his feet is on land and the other is dipping into the pool of water in front of him. He is perfectly balanced between both realms, patiently performing his endless task.

This card serves as a reminder to remain patient and go with the flow. You can't ever control a situation, but you can wait it out. You can't ever control other people, but you can be patient as they learn their own mistakes.

These are tough lessons to learn and even tougher to put into practice. The message of the Temperance card seems simple, but it is one of the strongest and most important cards in the deck.

In The Fool's journey through the Major Arcana, this card represents the lesson that change takes time. It's about acceptance, patience, and self-control.

Renewal and rejuvenation are coming, so don't go to extremes or force something to happen. Keep your focus on your values and don't let yourself be thrown off track by the influences of others, of your Ego, or of your base emotions.

KEYWORDS FOR THE TEMPERANCE TAROT CARD
Calm peacemaker
Economy, moderation, frugality
Finding the middle path
Exercise patience and self-control

KEYWORDS FOR THE TEMPERANCE REVERSED
Being out of balance
Doing things to excess
The church, religion

PATTERNS AND CORRESPONDENCES
Major Arcana = the lessons along your life's journey
Zodiac sign = Sagittarius, Cancer

TEMPERANCE READING FOR LOVE
Wait, wait, wait. This is not the time to search for new love, or try to bring an existing relationship closer together. Things will work themselves out, so step back and quit trying to force things. Enjoy the process and every moment you get to spend living your life, whether you are single or spending it together.

Go with the flow and maintain emotional balance. You might (gasp!) even be wrong about this situation, but with time you'll have the information you need. Don't go all crazy just yet.

Temperance Reading for Work

The Temperance card is sometimes called "the Peacemaker." Be the one who looks for the middle path or the win-win solution everyone can agree to.

Remain patient, even with the idiots who are running around trying to force things. Exercise self-control and moderation, keep your emotions in check, and remain above the drama. You'll end up in a much better place.

Not only will you feel better when you maintain this distance and your integrity, but your actions will be noticed by the mature players. Being in control of one's emotions is a high-level leadership skill.

Temperance Reading for Health

The Temperance card is great if you want to start doing yoga or Tai Chi. It's all about going with the flow.

It's also about moderation and balance. Don't go overboard on junk food or commit to losing ten pounds by the end of the month. Take things slowly and be patient. Be the turtle, not the hare.

There are no quick-fixes or magic pills that will get you healthy. You didn't get into this situation overnight, so don't expect an overnight change.

Make changes you can sustain for a lifetime and you will see lifetime change.

Temperance Reading for Money and Finances

The Temperance card is the opposite of a risk-taking card. It's about moderation and balance.

Money doesn't play well with emotional decisions. Money loves clarity, rational thought, and daily actions taken over the long-term. So take your time and be patient. There's no reason to rush.

Be patient with your investments and financial growth. You'll achieve far more through small daily actions than you will from one-time lottery wins. You need to create, cultivate, and practice good money habits before you will be able to handle big money windfalls.

TEMPERANCE READING FOR SPIRITUAL GUIDANCE

This feels like a very spiritual card (and it is), but it's also a very practical and mundane card, too.

The Temperance card guides you to wait, to be patient, and to go with the flow. Step back from the everyday hustle and put your life into balance.

There is no reason to rush this process. Your spiritual journey will last your entire lifetime. There is no end.

Pare your life down to its basics and you will find your true values. The key is to maintain those values as you consciously add people, activities, roles, and situations back into your life.

You get to create your own life, every bit of it. You can choose to create it based on your values and desires, or you can let life happen to you. Would you rather be in control of your life or a victim of your circumstances?

THE DEVIL

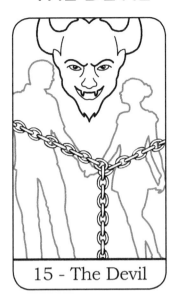

15 - The Devil

The Devil card represents temptation and indulgent sensual pleasures. You know it's bad for you, but it feels so very, very good.

This card is usually seen as a warning against obsessions, compulsions, and addictions. It is so easy to become a slave to the material and physical world. These desires can quickly turn toward greed, exploitation, and oppression.

Traditionally, this card card is visually similar to The Lovers. It shows a naked man and woman chained to a pillar. They are lorded over by a very large devil figure with bat wings, horns, and furry pants.

This isn't a negative card, though. You'll have to read the other cards around it to get a feel for the situation.

In a positive sense, you may need to start enjoying the pleasures of life. Let yourself become spontaneous and playful.

It might even be time to start exploring your deepest, naughtiest desires and participating in those pleasures without fear, shame, or excess.

Keywords for The Devil Tarot Card
Obsessive addiction
Bondage through greed, materialism, addiction
Let loose and enjoy the pleasures of life
Excessive sexual indulgence or other compulsive behaviors

Keywords for The Devil Reversed
Recovery, release, breaking free
Weakness, blindness
Reclaiming your power

Patterns and Correspondences
Major Arcana = the lessons of your life and personal growth
Zodiac sign = Capricorn, as Pan the hedonist

The Devil Reading for Love
Hmmm. Not much love here, but there's plenty of lust.

And lust can be good. As long as everyone involved is a consenting and willing adult and no one gets hurt (who doesn't want to), there's plenty of fun to be explored.

Just be careful. And don't let your kinks, fetishes, or whatevers take over your life or rule your happiness.

When you're in bondage to your desires, it can isolate you and separate you from others. And it's so easy for shame, guilt, fear, and excess slip in when you feel different, wrong, or embarrassed.

Explore, express, and accept yourself - all of yourself - without shame. You can do this exploration within a relationship, within many relationships, or alone.

The Devil Reading for Work
Are your dreams and desires only about financial or material success? If so, it's likely The Devil has taken over and made you a slave to your physical desires. You are a slave. You have created your own chains and you are the one who maintains them. Is this really how you want to live?

Money is good. So are fame and success. But when you let them rule your life at the expense of your happiness or the happiness of others, you're no longer in control.

The Devil card is a warning that your priorities are out of whack. Take control of your compulsive behaviors and free yourself from the limitations you are putting on yourself and your life.

THE DEVIL READING FOR HEALTH

This card is a strong indicator for addiction, obsession, and compulsive behaviors. Those are nothing to be ashamed of.

Really. Shame doesn't help. It isn't even real - it's a stupid belief you're carrying around that makes you feel even worse while you dig a deeper hole.

If you're worried about any behavior that feels out of your control, it's time to ask for help. Go see a professional or talk with someone you trust. Say the words out loud. Follow their advice, even if it seems stupid or pointless. And stop isolating yourself - this isn't something you can do on your own.

You may not see it right now, but what you're giving up is tiny compared to all of the things you're about to gain.

THE DEVIL READING FOR MONEY AND FINANCES

You spend too much money on stuff that doesn't matter. It doesn't even make you happy. Stop doing things that don't make you happy.

The Devil shines a light on your envy and greed. Your negativity is tainting your view of the world. Buying things you don't love to impress people you don't respect using money you don't have…it's not the smartest idea you've ever had. Why do you care about that shit in the first place?

Instead, be radical. Look deep within to find out what really matters to you. How you spend your money is a vote you make on what you want to exist in the world.

Do you want more beauty? Spend your money on art you love, flowers, and making yourself feel like a sexy goddess.

Do you want to be more connected to your family? Spend your money on picnics in the park, vacations, board games, or whatever gets you hanging out together.

Find out what matters to you, then direct all your excess resources to it. It's your money. You get to make the rules.

THE DEVIL READING FOR SPIRITUAL GUIDANCE

The Devil card is your friend. He's a reminder there's more to life than feeling good. And while everyone really enjoys feeling good, it's not always what you need.

Short-term pleasures often run counter to long-term contentment. Neither is right or wrong, or better than the other, but be clear which one you are choosing and be willing to pay the "tax" with whatever choice you make.

It's important to explore the dark side of your desires, without fear, shame, or excess. You can't unconditionally love yourself if you won't acknowledge your shadow side. That "bad stuff" is as much a part of you as your compassion, your sense of humor, and your nose.

Once you explore, acknowledge, and accept ALL parts of yourself, you have more control over which parts you allow to play.

You get to choose the forces that rule your life. For example, you don't let your nose make decisions or let it define you, do you? Then why should your addictions, compulsions, and obsessive behavior? Make peace with them, grab the reins, and move on.

THE TOWER

16 - The Tower

The Tower tarot card brings up strong emotions. It represents unexpected, unwanted, and unseen change. The Tower shows up when things are about to drastically change in your life.

Things are going to get worse before they get better.

The change is ultimately good, but some shit is about to go down before you get there. You are under attack from forces beyond your control or understanding. There is nothing you can do.

It's an unexpected attack, so you won't see it coming and you can't prepare for it.

With such a scary and unwanted meaning, many people consider this to be a "negative" card. However, there aren't really any negative cards in the tarot deck.

The Tower is necessary for change and growth. Ultimately, it has a powerful and inspiring message: there is something wonderful on the other side of this pain, but the only way out of this mess is to go through it.

In The Fool's journey through the Major Arcana, The Tower card represents the last of the major life lessons: you can't control everything and bad things happen to good people. That's a guarantee. Now, what are you going to do about it?

KEYWORDS FOR THE TOWER TAROT CARD
Sudden and unwanted breakthrough and change
Necessary upheaval or crisis
Under attack by forces beyond your control
Violence, hostile takeover

KEYWORDS FOR THE TOWER REVERSED
Fear of change
Stressing over nothing
Disaster has been averted
Listen to the rumblings of change and prepare

PATTERNS AND CORRESPONDENCES
Major Arcana = the lessons along your life's journey
Zodiac sign = Taurus, Aquarius
Planet = Mars

THE TOWER READING FOR LOVE
There's a dramatic upheaval about to happen in your love life.

The change will be BIG and unexpected. It might even be good.

But whatever happens will knock you on your ass and you won't be prepared for it. The best you can do is accept it when it comes and deal with it when it happens.

Don't assume the change will mean heartbreak and loneliness. It might, but no matter what change comes, this situation will ultimately be for the best. This is something you must go through to get to the true relationship you are meant to have.

The Tower Reading for Work

In a corporate or business setting, The Tower can indicate a hostile takeover or unwanted business interference. There are (usually unknown or unseen) outside forces attacking, causing you misery and distress, and possibly even ruining everything you've created.

There is sometimes an element of deception here, too.

But remember, this drastic upheaval is ultimately for the better. You will be forced to majorly shift your perspective about your work and your role in it.

Even though this change is not welcome, it is necessary and will result in a stronger business or career more in line with your values, passions, and talents. This awful thing that feels like "the end of the world" is actually one of the best things that could happen to you!

The Tower Reading for Health

This is not a great card if you're trying to get or stay healthy. You (or your body) is under attack from outside forces. It's time to rally the troops and address the situation as quickly as you can. This is your Rock Bottom.

This means you need to immediately schedule a full medical exam, including blood work and appropriate tests. Visit the dentist and whatever other medical professionals you use and trust.

Definitely get a second opinion about any negative or questionable results and trust your gut. If something feels wrong, it probably is.

When it comes to losing weight or taking medications, be extremely cautious. You might be sold some snake-oil or other useless (or even harmful) solutions. Getting healthy - truly healthy - isn't quick or easy. Don't be swindled into believing otherwise.

Rarely, this card indicates actual physical violence or abuse.

The Tower Reading for Money and Finances

Financially, there is nothing good about The Tower. Be as conservative as you can with your finances right now. There's some major upheaval coming and you can't do anything to control or predict it.

Ultimately, this change is for the best, however, so don't despair. Things will work out, just not how you planned.

This is definitely not the time to be making any investments, redistributions, or committing to big expenses.

If you are in partnership with anyone, personally or professionally, it is your responsibility to fully understand all of your shared financials. There may be something underhanded or sneaky happening and you will be blindsided by the betrayal when it comes to light.

Protect yourself the best you can by refusing to sign any document you don't fully understand and by asking questions until you feel 100% confident you understand the answer. Don't be bullied by someone who "knows better" than you about this stuff. No one is born understanding how money works. This is a skill you can learn with study and concentrated effort.

The Tower Reading for Spiritual Guidance

The Tower card is sometimes called "the Liberator." It frees you from your chains, your past, your hopes, your expectations, and everything you thought you wanted.

You are being given the opportunity to start over and recreate yourself from scratch. What a wonderful opportunity!

Even though this card is an omen of unwanted change, everything about this change is ultimately good. A major, and necessary, shift in your perspective is coming. Be open to all ideas and everything else coming your way.

This will change your life. And you will (ultimately) be grateful.

THE STAR

17 - The Star

The Star tarot card is sometimes called "the fairy godmother" card, because it arrives to let you know everything is going to work out fine. This is very good news, especially after the upheaval of The Tower, which proceeds it.

In the Fool's Journey through the Major Arcana, The Star is paired with The Moon and The Sun. Together these three cards wrap up the climax of our quest and start to bring us back to where we started, only as completely changed individuals.

This card takes the turmoil of The Tower and turns that energy into renewal, hope, and peace. In the RW-based tradition, The Star shows a naked woman pouring one jug of water into a pond, while she pours another jug onto the ground. Eight stars shine down, lighting the world around her.

Unlike the moon and the sun, the stars are lighting up the sky above us even when we don't see them. You don't need to believe in them to make them exist. They are always there, no matter what you think or do.

The Universe has your back in the same way that the stars shine during the day. You don't need to believe in the support of the Universe for it to exist. The support is always there, no matter what you think or do.

Have faith and believe that things are going to be okay, or even better than okay. They always have been and they always will be.

Sometimes, The Star is a bit of a "show business" card, too. If you've ever wanted to see your name in lights, it's time to take center stage. Be authentically you and let your true light shine through.

Keywords for The Star Tarot Card
Renewal, hope, healing
All is calm and clear
Have faith, believe in miracles
Unexpected help

Keywords for The Star Reversed
Fear takes over
Depression, illness, impotence
Arrogance, despair

Patterns and Correspondences
Major Arcana = your life's journey and spiritual growth
Zodiac sign = Aquarius

The Star Reading for Love
The Star is a positive card in a love reading, especially if you've had difficulties in your relationship or in finding a good partner.

The key is to be yourself and to have faith that you are enough, exactly as you are. To succeed with a healthy and loving relationship, you need to bring all the good and all the not-so-good bits of yourself into view. No more hiding or pretending to be someone you're not.

If you are looking for new love, put on your sparkliest outfit and get out there. You need to shine to be seen, so make sure you are mingling and meeting people. Never give up faith. When the time is right for you both, you will meet your perfect partner.

THE STAR READING FOR WORK

This card shows up in a reading when things are going to get better. If you've been struggling at work or with finding the perfect career path, things are on the way up. Don't give up hope!

The Universe wants you to be of service to the world. It needs you to be your strongest, bravest, and best self.

Concentrate on letting yourself shine. Don't hide your best assets or apologize for who you are and what you desire.

You have very bright prospects, but you have to be visible and seen to make things happen. Get out there and keep the faith.

THE STAR READING FOR HEALTH

This is a great card for healing and renewal. If you've had health problems, it looks like they are going to resolve themselves positively.

To take better care of your health, consider meditation and stress-relieving activities. You've been under a lot of pressure lately, so put yourself at the center of your life and get your own needs met.

No matter how scary, awful, or frustrating things have been, you are on the way back to solid good health. Visualizing yourself as a healthy person and truly believing good health is possible are requirements. If you stay stuck in fear, confusion, or frustration, you will never improve.

THE STAR READING FOR MONEY AND FINANCES

The Star points out areas that need a bit of light, so if you've been ignoring financial matters, address them. Take a good hard and honest look at your money situation. Shine a light on everything, just as The Star would.

Things will work out but you can no longer hide from the truth.

Fretting, worrying, and stressing about money will not help you. Clarity, acceptance, and a plan will. Adjust your attitude and stay positive.

Even in the worst financial pits, there are still many things to be grateful for. Begin a daily Gratitude Journal to note all of the wonderful things you do have in your life. It's impossible to stay stuck in lack once you realize how full your life actually is!

Don't rely on it, but you may be the recipient of unseen and unexpected help. Be open to receiving this gift and don't push it away.

THE STAR READING FOR SPIRITUAL GUIDANCE

Everyone's spiritual journey is different, but we end up in the same place. (Unfortunately, it's a place filled with cliches that don't mean anything until you've walked the path yourself)!

Phrases like "you already have everything you need," and "you are one with the Universe" sound hokey until you internalize them.

Ultimately, the thing you've been searching for is…YOU.

It's not about learning something new to become a better version of yourself. It's about learning how to bring yourself - your full sell - into everything you think, say, and do.

Once you realize this, then the hard work begins!

THE MOON

18 - The Moon

The Moon tarot card follows the hope, faith, and trust of The Star, to point out things may not be as they seem. It's not about having blind faith. This is about the faith that comes from trusting and following your own values and intuition.

Be on the lookout for unseen problems, deceptions, and haters. You could easily let your imagination and subconscious take you to dark and unfriendly places, so keep your anxiety in check.

Proceed with caution and prudence, but always let your intuition be your guide. This card is a very strong call to trust yourself.

Pay attention to what isn't said or what isn't seen. Your imagination and creativity will guide you.

Use a dream journal beside your bed to write down your dreams as soon as you wake. Your subconscious is trying to tell you something and your dreams are its language. Look for the patterns, memories, and flashes of inspiration that come to you at night.

In traditional RW-based decks, The Moon card shows a tame dog and a wild wolf howling at the moon. There's a water scorpion (or lobster or crawfish) climbing out of the water in front of them. The moon is combined with the sun and is centered between two towers.

As The Fool begins to wrap up his journey through the Major Arcana, The Moon (along with The Star and The Sun) represent the process of internalizing the lessons of the previous cards. While The Star is about trusting the Universe, The Moon is about trusting yourself.

KEYWORDS FOR THE MOON TAROT CARD
Slow down and pay attention to your intuition
Follow your intuition, imagination, and dreams
Proceed with caution
An unclear and difficult path lies ahead

KEYWORDS FOR THE MOON REVERSED
Truths are revealed
Good common sense prevails
No more hiding or fear

PATTERNS AND CORRESPONDENCES
Major Arcana = the arc of your life's lessons and spiritual growth
Zodiac sign = Pisces
Planet = the Moon, of course
Element = Water

THE MOON READING FOR LOVE
If you are looking for a new relationship, proceed with caution and trust your intuition. If things don't feel right, they probably aren't.

When meeting new people and dating, pay attention to the things your partner isn't saying or isn't asking you. There is as much, if not more, information in what is hidden as there is in what is said.

Notice whether their actions match their words. If their stories or explanations don't make sense, trust your gut and walk away. This process of dating is not about whether or not they like you, it's completely about whether or not you like them. If they aren't 100% awesome and admirable, don't waste your time.

If you are in an existing relationship, look deeper. Things may not be as they seem on the surface. This doesn't necessarily mean cheating, lying, or affairs. Your partner may just be keeping something quiet because they are afraid of being judged or abandoned.

Investigate deep within yourself to get clear on your own desires. Be honest about your relationship's strengths, weaknesses, and future prospects. Trust your intuition and take your time when making decisions.

Ultimately, this is your life and you are the only one that matters. (Yes! Even if there are children involved. Do what's best for yourself without causing danger or harm to anyone else.)

The Moon Reading for Work

This is a particularly good card for creative problem solving. Use your intuition, creativity, and imagination for new solutions.

Shrug off outside pressure and trust your knowledge, skills, talents, and experience. You know what to do, so trust yourself and don't keep your solutions to yourself.

If you are having problems at work, there is something unsaid or unknown about the situation. When moving forward, proceed with extreme caution and be very careful about what you do and say.

Watch out for awful coworkers or colleagues who may be jealous about your success and skills. If they are talking behind your back, they may be creating bigger problems you will have to clean up later.

Don't let your anxiety get the best of you, though. Things aren't necessarily negative. They are simply unseen and unknown.

The Moon Reading for Health

The Moon card is pushing you to visit your doctor for a full physical. There may be something going on that doesn't have any clear symptoms. It's always good to get a clean bill of health.

This card sometimes points to issues with shame, intoxication, or denial. If you have problems with addiction or compulsion with a substance or behavior, it's time to address those issues.

You already know if you have a problem. No matter how scary seems, things will improve if you let yourself be humble and ask for the help you need.

The Moon Reading for Money and Finances

There will be a slow and difficult path ahead. If you are contemplating a major financial decision, take a deeper look at the situation. What is your gut telling you?

Money is a tool that amplifies everything around it. Money intensifies fears and emotions.

If you are creative, having more money will allow you to be more creative. If you are fearful, having more money will increase your anxiety.

What does money currently amplify in your life? Is this what you want to see growing?

The Moon Reading for Spiritual Guidance

It's time to investigate your spiritual beliefs.

Meditation, journaling, and recording your dreams are great places to start and it doesn't have to take much time each day.

The Moon represents voluntary and positive change. Slow down and center yourself during whatever moments of solitude you can find throughout your day. Listen to the quiet voice coming from your center. The more you listen to it, the louder and more clear it will become.

THE SUN

19 - The Sun

Traditionally, The Sun tarot card shows a very happy child riding a horse and holding a flag. Behind the child is a large sun and a garden of sunflowers.

It's an extremely positive card, especially for marriage, children, or material success. This is an active card about celebrating how far you've come. Things are going extremely well, so take the time to show gratitude with a sense of child-like wonder.

As The Fool wraps up his journey through the Major Arcana, The Sun has a clear and positive message about the connection between a fun, positive attitude and good health, happiness, and success. You have done the hard work to learn and integrate this life lesson. Now it's time to honor and mark your growth.

The Sun card doesn't want you to wait, either. Celebrating and showing gratitude for your success is mandatory. Don't put it off or immediately start striving for something better. This is a wonderful time and deserves to be honored as such.

You've come so far and are amazing! When you recognize and

acknowledge your accomplishments, you allow even more wonderful things to happen.

KEYWORDS FOR THE SUN TAROT CARD
Celebration, pleasure, and abundance
Good health, material happiness
Child-like wonder and joy
A fortunate marriage or the birth of a beloved child

KEYWORDS FOR THE SUN REVERSED
Temporary depression or lack of success
Delayed gratification
Kids behaving badly

PATTERNS AND CORRESPONDENCES
Major Arcana = the arc of your life's journey
Zodiac sign = Leo
Planet = the Sun, of course

THE SUN READING FOR LOVE
This is a wonderful card for love! If you are looking for a new relationship, true love is coming to you.

You are fully deserving of unconditional, intimate, healthy, and committed romantic love. You are so loving and so lovable! Get ready to be adored by your perfect romantic partner.

And if you are hoping to deepen your existing relationship, either with a marriage proposal or children, this is a wonderful card to see in a tarot reading.

THE SUN READING FOR WORK
The Sun card indicates material happiness, success, growth, and honors. It is a very positive card for work and career.

If you are looking for a promotion, ask for a big one! With any raise or promotion, ask for a dollar figure that represents your true value to the company, not something based on cost-of-living raises or your needs.

You are fully deserving of being paid well for a job you do so well.

If you are searching for a new job, you can expect help from unexpected sources and success. Your perfect job is already working its way into your life. Be ready to pounce when it becomes available.

THE SUN READING FOR HEALTH

All is well. If you have been struggling with health problems, The Sun is shining down with bright happiness on your recovery.

This is a celebratory and active card, so get moving! To get and stay healthy, spend time playing like children do. Fun activities, especially outdoors, are wonderful for your physical and mental health.

Overall, you need more fun in your life. We all do!

So start adding little bits of fun and joy into your days. Put on music as you do the dishes and dance. Wear a wig and sequins to the grocery store. Eat off the good china, every damn day. You deserve it!

THE SUN READING FOR MONEY AND FINANCES

Material success and abundance are coming. If you've had money troubles in the past, they will soon be over.

Watch out for help from unexpected sources. The Universe wants you to be rich and will keep sending money your way. Say yes to all of it, bless it, and send it on to do good works. You're such an abundantly good steward of this flow!

Keep being smart with your money. And most of all, give yourself credit for how much you've learned and grown over the last few years. You have created your own luck and success.

THE SUN READING FOR SPIRITUAL GUIDANCE

The Universe is glowing with you. You have come so far along your spiritual journey that the person you once were is barely recognizable to the person you have become.

Take some time to reflect on how much you've changed. Be sure to give yourself credit for doing the hard work of transformation!

No one else could have done this for you and you were so brave. You kept doing the work even when it was scary, dark, and lonely. You're just amazing. Absolutely wonderfully awesome. Yay, you!

Honor your journey with a memento, tattoo, piece of jewelry, or beautiful work of art. You aren't done growing yet, of course, but who you are now definitely deserves recognition and celebration.

JUDGMENT

20 - Judgment

The Judgment card has a big message for you. You can no longer hide or ignore the truths of your life. It's not possible to pretend any more.

You see clearly. You know exactly what your passions, desires, and values are. You know your place in the world and how you can best serve.

And with this information, you can't stay stuck. You have no choice but to remove everything that no longer fits with who you are and move into living the life you were meant to live.

This card is a huge wakeup call for renewal and transformation.

In traditional RW-based tarot decks, the Judgment tarot card shows the archangel Gabriel blowing on his horn, calling the dead out of their coffins. They rise up to him with their arms outstretched.

It's kind of creepy to see all the dead people, but this card isn't about "The Judgment" or "The Rapture" in the traditional religious sense. In fact, the message of this card is completely universal.

You see the greater purpose in your life and have learned through all the mistakes you've made. It's time to move on and move forward. You are being called toward something bigger.

In The Fool's journey through the Major Arcana, this card begins to outline the lessons for your next cycle.

Life is a constant cycle of learning and transformation. You've completely learned the previous lessons you needed to learn. Now it is about stepping up to live as a wiser, more powerful, and more whole version of yourself.

KEYWORDS FOR THE JUDGMENT TAROT CARD
A big wakeup call
Take action on your truth
A new day starts
A final decision or sentencing

KEYWORDS FOR THE JUDGMENT CARD REVERSED
Denial or ignorance
An error in judgment
Being judged unfairly

PATTERNS AND CORRESPONDENCES
Major Arcana = your life's journey of growth and transformation
Zodiac sign = Scorpio
Planet = Pluto
Element = Fire

THE JUDGMENT READING FOR LOVE
Something isn't working and you can't pretend anymore.

If you are looking for new love, your tactics and efforts have been weak and ineffective. You can do better. Toot your own horn and get out there!

If you are in a relationship, you need to do an internal review and assess whether you are working together as partners or are on different paths.

Anticipate a wakeup call and a fresh start. There is no room for the same-old-thing anymore. And frankly, you don't want it anyway. You've grown and aren't willing to put up with a partner who isn't growing as well.

THE JUDGMENT READING FOR WORK

You are being called to something bigger. You have a bigger purpose in life than what you have been doing.

Dig deep to find your true passions, desires, values, and talents. Once you know your truth, you can no longer live any other way.

This card can indicate a change in position or a new start.

You may be promoted, let go, or fired from your current position. If that happens, it's definitely for the best.

Consider this situation a wake-up call to take charge of your career. You don't need another just-paying-the-bills job. It's time to devote yourself to the work you are being called to do.

THE JUDGMENT READING FOR HEALTH

If you've been lying to yourself (or others) about your health situation, come clean and get honest.

You are done with shame, embarrassment, and fear. You don't have time for them anymore. You're too focused on healing yourself with compassion, integrity, and faith.

You know things will change for the better, but only when you change.

Every bit of extra time, focus, and energy is now devoted to healing your body, your mind, and your soul. It's the only thing that matters.

THE JUDGMENT READING FOR MONEY AND FINANCES

The Judgment card sometimes anticipates a loss through a lawsuit, or a final decision or sentencing. Do an internal audit of your finances to see if you are in danger of losing money through bad investments, debts, or past mistakes.

Come clean and clear up your mess before it catches up with you. Take control, be humble, and do the work to regain the trust you've lost.

If you've been spending more than you'd like, the pattern can't continue. There is only one way to get out of debt and it requires you to stop spending more than you are earning. You need to face this fact and align your choices with reality.

Pretending things will work out somehow isn't a plan. Neither is avoidance, denial, or blame. Take charge of your own mess and clean it up yourself. No one can do this for you.

The Judgment Reading for Spiritual Guidance
You are being called to something bigger. Much, much, much bigger.

The Judgment card, at least in the traditional RW-based tarot deck, has strong religious vibes, but it doesn't mean you are being called to a specific religion. It doesn't mean you are going to be "judged" or "condemned" because of your beliefs (or lack of them), either.

Instead, it's about being called to step up into your own power. You know your deepest truth and you must follow it.

In the past, you could have ignored this calling. Not any more. It isn't possible for you to pretend, hide, or live in denial any longer.

Now, you are completely unwilling to live your life as a lie. It just isn't possible. The only option for you is to live your life aligned with your truth, damn the consequences.

You aren't afraid (much) and you are 100% willing to take responsibility for this decision. It's full-speed-ahead into your new life!

THE WORLD

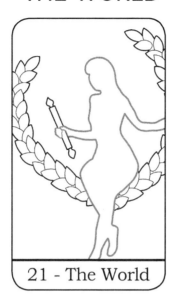

21 - The World

The World tarot card is the last card of the Major Arcana. You've reached the end of one journey and are ready to begin another.

Traditionally, The World card shows a naked woman wrapped in a banner and holding two double-ended candles. She floats in the center of a wreath surrounded by heads of the fixed signs of the zodiac – a bull for Taurus, a lion for Leo, an eagle for Scorpio, and a water-bearer for Aquarius.

Along The Fool's journey through the Major Arcana, this is a card of closure. You have fulfilled your purpose and goal.

Now it's time to start another one.

Sometimes that means beginning again with The Fool and traveling through the Major Arcana, either learning a new lesson or experiencing the same lesson at a deeper level.

And, sometimes, it means going on an adventure! This is a great card if you are want to take a long trip or relocate to another location. All signs are positive for your new adventure.

Keywords for The World Tarot Card
Culmination of all your skills and efforts
Completion of a major life lesson
Self-actualization
Flight, moving, international travel

Keywords for The World Reversed
Inertia, permanence
Unfinished lessons
Problems while traveling

Patterns and Correspondences
Major Arcana = the cycle of your journey and spiritual growth
Zodiac sign = Capricorn
Planet = Saturn

The World Reading for Love
If you are in a long-distance relationship, consider relocating to be with your love. You might have to make the move (not them). It will absolutely be worth it!

If you are in a relationship with problems, you may have gone as far as you can with your current relationship or situation. You've reached the peak!

This may be good or bad news depending on your desires, but it's unlikely to change. You have completed a major life lesson and closure is coming.

If you are looking for a new relationship, you are ready to put yourself out there. Specifically, hang out in the places where you will find the type of partner you want to have.

If you're looking for someone who loves to travel, start traveling. If you want a family-focused partner, hang out with your friends who have kids. And if you're looking for someone athletic, start participating in the sports and activities you enjoy.

THE WORLD READING FOR WORK

You have reached the end of the road as far as your current position. You've learned everything you can and it's time to move on.

This might mean you need to leave your job or sell your business. But it could also mean you need to seek out new responsibilities, different types of projects, or clients who are more in line with your interests.

When it comes to this change, think as big as you can and then think even bigger.

If you are looking for a promotion, advancement, or even an overseas assignment, this is the time to ask for what you want. You'll probably get it!

THE WORLD READING FOR HEALTH

You need to challenge your body in new ways. What used to work for you is not working any longer.

Maybe you've gotten older and your metabolism is junk. Maybe you've plateaued on your weight loss or athletic training. Whatever your situation, you will have to try a new path.

But first, give credit to yourself for making it this far.

Mourn what you've lost, if you must. Then start experimenting and exploring to find the new actions that work for you. This is a grand new adventure and you will find success.

THE WORLD READING FOR MONEY AND FINANCES

Congratulations! You are very close to reaching your financial goals.

Keep up the good work and don't go crazy. But it looks like you'll soon be celebrating, perhaps with a nice vacation to someplace overseas?

The World is an adventurous card, so take some risks with your money. (Only the money you can afford to lose, of course!)

This isn't about trying to win the lottery or playing high-stakes poker. Instead, invest your money in the dreams of your friends, family, and community. You may not make huge financial returns, but you will be able to create real change in the world you live in.

THE WORLD READING FOR SPIRITUAL GUIDANCE

The Major Arcana is a cycle. As soon as you learn one life's lesson, you are right back to being The Fool.

It may feel like you have reached "heaven on earth" and are ready to rest on your laurels, but this is only a resting place. If you stay stuck here, you will become bitter, dissatisfied, and stagnant.

After you rest, celebrate, and honor your achievements, you must move on to the next goal or challenge you've set for yourself. Life is a continuous cycle of learning, change, growth, evolution, and transformation.

You will continue to cycle through the cards as you dive deeper into the person you are meant to become. Each time you work your way through the Major Arcana's cycle, you will be creating (and re-creating) the world you want to live in, in your own image.

ACE OF CUPS

Ace of Cups

The Ace of Cups represents true love and emotional fulfillment. But unlike a lot of the emotional Cups cards, this one is very active. It's about making things happen.

So, while it may indicate an outpouring of love is coming your way, it could also mean YOU are the one who needs to take a big emotional risk and ask for what you want.

Open your heart to love and be vulnerable. It's the scariest thing of them all, but it's also the only way to get the healthy, fulfilling, and abundant love you desire. The Ace of Cups is a bit like the Holy Grail. It represents the true love and emotional fulfillment everyone is searching for.

This is a great card for relationships, both new ones and anyone looking to take the "next step." It's also a great card for babies. Lots and lots of babies.

In the traditional RW-based deck, the Ace of Cups shows a hand coming out of the sky, holding a goblet overflowing with water. A dove is dropping a wafer into the cup.

Unlike a lot of the emotional Cups cards, this one is very active and yang. It's about making things happen.

So, while it may indicate an outpouring of love is coming your way, it could also mean you are the one who needs to take a big emotional risk and ask for what you want.

Open your heart to love and be vulnerable. It's the scariest thing of them all, but it's also the only way to get the healthy, fulfilling, and abundant love you desire.

All of the Aces (with the number 1) represent new beginnings and the start of things. When you combine beginnings with the emotional element of the Cups, you get a new relationship, a new start in an existing relationship (like a proposal or a wedding), a new baby, a new creative project, or a new, fresh start.

KEYWORDS FOR THE ACE OF CUPS TAROT CARD
New love or attraction
Proposal, marriage, a wedding
Pregnancy or the birth of a child
Love, healing, abundance

KEYWORDS FOR THE ACE OF CUPS REVERSED
Emotional disappointments
Too much too soon
Feeling let down in a relationship

PATTERNS AND CORRESPONDENCES
The Cups suit = rules the emotions
Suit of cards = hearts
Timeline = weeks to months
Number 1 = new beginnings, starting on a journey
Element = Water

Ace of Cups Reading for Love

The Ace of Cups is one of the best cards to show up in a tarot reading about love. This is a fantastic card for both new relationships and for new starts in existing relationships.

If you are looking for a new relationship, things look extremely positive. You will have to do the work, of course, but keep your eyes out and your heart open, and you will shortly find someone wonderful.

In an existing relationship, expect something new and positive. This could be a huge leap forward in the level of your commitment, a chance to start over, or a new role for you to play. Whatever happens, it will be positive. The Ace of Cups also anticipates big emotional events, like engagements, weddings, pregnancies, and births.

Ace of Cups Reading for Work

If you work closely with others, you may experience a new beginning to your relationship with them. This doesn't necessarily mean a romantic relationship, although it is possible. You might also get new co-workers, a new boss, or new clients.

If you are looking for a new job, new position, or new approach in your business, this is a very positive and abundant card. It indicates an excellent opportunity is coming your way.

Ace of Cups Reading for Health

Joy, love, and healing are all indicated by the Ace of Cups. It's a positive card for health matters, especially anything dealing with fertility, pregnancy, and birth. Of course, you can't just sit and wish for things to happen. Babies get made - so get to work!

No matter what your situation and desires, you will have to take the first step to making your dreams happen. Sign up for a new class at the gym, hire a healthy meal-delivery service, or join a community of people who share your goals.

Whatever you need to do, take the first step.

Ace of Cups Reading for Money and Finances

The Ace of Cups is a very positive card, but be careful. Don't let your enthusiasm and emotions rule your head.

Although this card indicates abundance is coming, it's also a very active card. You're going to have to work for it!

You can expect money to flow your way, but this won't be lottery winnings or gifts. The money you'll receive will come from a new source, but it will be a source you created or initiated.

And this would be a perfect time to set up a new savings account, start a new budgeting program like YNAB, or meet with a financial planner for the first time. You need a new, fresh start with your finances.

Ace of Cups Reading for Spiritual Guidance

The dove on the Ace of Cups card symbolizes the spirit or the Divine, carrying a message from the Universe about your soul and your deepest desires.

Open your heart and be vulnerable. This means looking at and accepting yourself 100%. If you can't love yourself unconditionally, how do you expect to understand what that kind of love entails?

Your capacity to love - and to be loved - is endless. What would happen if you loved yourself without judgment, criticism, or fear?

TWO OF CUPS

2 of Cups

Everyone LOVES the Two of Cups tarot card. This is the Love Card, after all. But it is about much more than romantic love. It's a very positive card when dealing with any relationship pairing or partnership.

This card strongly indicates romance, attraction, and love. In situations where romance isn't the focus, it can also mean a strong business partnership, friendship, or other relationship between two parties.

In traditional RW-based decks, the Two of Cups shows a man and a woman, each holding a cup, reaching toward each other. A winged lion floats in the sky above them, protecting and blessing their relationship.

It's a particularly good card when trying to build a shared understanding or when you are working toward a common goal.

This definitely isn't a casual, fun and sexy-times pairing or a friends-with-benefits situation. The Two of Cups tarot card indicates a stronger, more solid relationship. (Of course, it can also mean a strong physical attraction, so maybe fun and sexy-times will be a part of it)!

Keywords for the Two of Cups Tarot Card
Love, romance, attraction
Relationships, partnerships
Shared understanding and support
Engagement, marriage

Keywords for the Two of Cups Reversed
Misunderstandings and arguments
A breakup or separation
Disinterest

Patterns and Correspondences
The Cups suit = rules the emotions
Suit of cards = hearts
Timeline = weeks to months
Number 2 = balance and pairings
Zodiac sign = Cancer
Element = Water

Two of Cups Reading for Love
Overall, the Two of Cups is a great card for love, romance, and attraction.

If you are looking for a new relationship, this is one of the very best cards for a solid long-term partnership. This will be a relationship that lasts.

If you are looking for something fun and casual like a vacation fling, this card anticipates something more. Your one-night-stand might turn into your dream partner or a friend you have for life.

If you are currently in a relationship, a marriage proposal or similar declaration of commitment is quite the possibility!

It's also a good card if you need to heal your relationship or are looking to reconcile your differences and move on to something deeper.

Two of Cups Reading for Work

This is a fantastic card for a business partnership. You are both on the same page and want the same things for this venture. Together, your strengths and weaknesses are complimentary. This is definitely a situation where One + One is greater than Two.

And if you haven't found your perfect partner yet, it looks like they will be arriving into your life soon.

In the office, any partnership looks golden. Don't be afraid to team up on a project to get the job done. Reach out to someone you admire and offer to help them with a specific task. Treat yourself as their peer and you'll become one.

Two of Cups Reading for Health

The Two of Cups is a very positive card for health and healing, especially when it comes to emotional wounds.

If your heart is broken or you are holding on to resentments from the past, you'll soon have the motivation and support to heal and move on. Moving through loss and grief takes time, but you're not the only one who has gone through this experience. Be vulnerable in sharing with others who have had similar experiences. Ask for help and support during this trying time and partner up with someone you trust.

If you are struggling with your physical or mental health, you have (or soon will have) the support you need. But any partnership requires the efforts of both parties to make it work, so it is your responsibility to step up and make changes in your life. You need to give as much as you gain and your actions will be a role model for your partner.

Two of Cups Reading for Money and Finances

This card, although overwhelmingly positive, doesn't indicate money coming into your life through luck or outside events. It's a card for sharing and working with a partner toward a common goal.

Whether in your personal or professional life, you need to get on the same page, financially-speaking, with your partner. If you two are working toward a goal (like saving for a house or paying off debt), it appears you will make things happen together.

Work together on this goal with honest communication and regular updates. Hold each other accountable with positive support, an open heart, and cheerful encouragement.

TWO OF CUPS READING FOR SPIRITUAL GUIDANCE

No one walks through this world alone. Even at our most isolated and alone, we are still connected to others through our memories, communities, and future possibilities.

Your energy and your existence connects you to everyone and everything else in the Universe. You are never alone.

As you investigate and discover your place in the world, you will meet other people who share similar beliefs, values, and stories. These people are your Tribe.

This card is a reminder that two people are always stronger, smarter, and more powerful than one. Although your spiritual journey is yours alone, you won't find meaning or purpose until you share your experiences with others. Compassion, generosity, kindness, trust, and honest communication are required practices along the path to enlightenment, and they can only be practiced through interaction with others.

THREE OF CUPS

3 of Cups

The Three of Cups tarot card is such a fun card! It's about celebrating the good things in your life with the people you love.

Traditionally, this card shows three happy women in a garden, dancing and holding their cups into the air. It's a party. They are in their own world and are having a blast.

It's a great card for engagements and weddings and also for holidays, parties, and other fun group events.

But it's not just about celebrating the good times. It's about celebrating the good times with the people who matter most to you. It's a card about community and support.

The Three of Cups is a fantastic card to see when you are feeling alone, stagnant, or unloved. It's basically telling you to rally the troops, throw a party, and get your groove back on!

KEYWORDS FOR THE THREE OF CUPS TAROT CARD
Celebrations, parties, fun
Friendship and support
Holidays, weddings, engagements
Enjoy this "honeymoon" period

KEYWORDS FOR THE THREE OF CUPS REVERSED
A love triangle
A romantic affair
"Three's a crowd"
It's time to apologize and make amends

PATTERNS AND CORRESPONDENCES
The Cups suit = rules the emotions
Suit of cards = hearts
Timeline = weeks to months
Number 3 = celebrating reality
Zodiac sign = Cancer
Element = Water

THREE OF CUPS READING FOR LOVE
This is such a great card for love, especially if you want to see your relationship formalized through some sort of partnership celebration (i.e. a proposal or wedding or handfasting). This card is about rejoicing in togetherness!

If you are single and looking for love, you need to use your circle of support. Ask your friends to set you up with people they think might be compatible. Make the effort to attend events where you might meet someone new. Throw a dinner party for all of your single friends and have them bring another single friend outside of your normal social circle. See who hits it off!

If your relationship is rocky, this card can occasionally mean "three's a crowd," especially when reversed. There may be a secret third party you don't know about or you could be involved with someone who is threatening your current relationship. This card can also indicate a love-triangle or throuple (a three-way couple) situation.

Three of Cups Reading for Work

Celebrate your professional accomplishments, big and small. You are accomplishing great things, so celebrate those happy times, especially with other coworkers. And be sure to celebrate their successes as well!

If there is a challenging situation at work, you'll need to solve these problems by working together with others. This isn't a time to go off on your own, lone-wolf style.

Use your network, your mastermind, and your circles of support to master this situation. Then throw a party to celebrate when the project is finished! You all deserve it.

Three of Cups Reading for Health

This is a very positive card for matters of health and your body. If you are facing health problems, use your friends, family, and health professionals to create a circle of support around you.

If you are looking to improve your health in general, look for activities involving others. Group classes, sports, classroom-style lessons, and shared meals would be a wonderful way to explore treating your body better.

Share what you are learning. The best way to learn something new and cement it as a habit is to teach it to others.

Three of Cups Reading for Money and Finances

The Three of Cups card indicates abundance and pleasure as well as celebrations and fun.

If you've been keeping a tight grip on your finances, don't forget to spend a bit on yourself. You don't need to go hog-wild, but treat yourself as well as (or even better than) the way you treat your loved ones.

If money is currently tight, things will be getting better in the future. Until then, continue to treat yourself well, without going into debt or blowing money you need elsewhere. Most of life's little pleasures can be experienced at little cost. Notice and celebrate all of the wonderful things already in your life by keeping a Gratitude Journal and sharing what you have with open-hearted generosity.

THREE OF CUPS READING FOR SPIRITUAL GUIDANCE

Jesus turned water into wine because he wanted to throw a grand party and show the power of belief. Following your spiritual path, whether it aligns with traditional religion or not, is supposed to be FUN!

Find or create a circle of support and encouragement for yourself as you explore your place and purpose in the world.

The journey you take is yours alone and no one can do the work for you. But you won't get very far if you don't involve others and you won't stay committed to the process if you don't have fun!

FOUR OF CUPS

4 of Cups

The traditional RW image on the Four of Cups tarot card is strange. What is that hand doing? Where is it coming from???

You've got a guy so focused on what's directly in front of him that he doesn't see the disembodied zombie hand coming out of the sky! That's such an apt way of depicting this message, which is about feeling so unfulfilled and bored with your life you've become blind to the gifts and opportunities in front of you.

This card is about pulling away from the "normal" day-to-day and focusing on the wild and creative part of you that sits deep inside instead.

The way to cure your apathy and ennui is by diving within yourself to identify your core values, passions, and desires and then bring your anchored sense of identity to life with passion and enthusiasm without caring about what anyone else thinks. When you are on the right path, you'll can grab at the synchronicities and gifts in front of you to create your own opportunities.

Keywords for the Four of Cups Tarot Card
Boredom, apathy, feeling unfulfilled
Meditation, withdrawal, looking within
An unexpected offering
A missed opportunity or blind spot

Keywords for the Four of Cups Reversed
A breakthrough
A new outlook or direction
New and unexpected creative ideas

Patterns and Correspondences
The Cups suit = rules the emotions
Suit of cards = hearts
Timeline = weeks to months
Number 4 = practical foundations
Zodiac sign = Cancer
Element = Water

Four of Cups Reading for Love
In all cases, the Four of Cups card is telling you to go inside for your answers and to put into action what you see there.

Love yourself unconditionally so you can show the same depth of love to others. Be open to receiving the love that is given to you with a receptive awareness and a clear heart.

If you are having relationship problems, first realize you can't change anyone else. You can only change your own thoughts, words, and behaviors. Look within yourself to see what part you play in these patterns. (If you feel stuck, journaling, role-playing, and therapy really help).

And if you are looking for a new relationship, you may be overlooking someone who is right under your nose! Instead of looking for your "ideal" mate or the "right" person, take a clear inventory of the wonderful people already in your life. Don't be so blinded by what you don't have that you miss out on what you do.

Four of Cups Reading for Work

If you are feeling bored and dissatisfied with your job, it's time to change something up!

Start by asking yourself some tough questions: Are you truly living the life you imagined for yourself? Or have you settled for what was easiest or expected of you?

Identify one simple and tiny change you could take to get yourself closer to your ideal situation. Then take action and turn that one step into reality.

This is not the time to barrel gung-ho into a new project or activity. Instead, take it slow. Spend time quietly contemplating and exploring your options. Make one small step and then re-evaluate. It is your responsibility to understand everything happening in your environment before you make a permanent decision. You don't want to miss that creepy hand coming at you!

Four of Cups Reading for Health

Take time to nurture yourself. When it comes to your health, there may be many options you aren't seeing or considering. Explore ALL of your options before making a decision.

The Four of Cups is a reminder that we can get so lost in our fears and expectations we miss out on what's sitting right in front of our face. Take a good look at your environment, your habits, your support circles, and your daily activities.

Consider the small steps you could take toward greater health and take action on the first small change. Watch out for synchronicities and opportunities that seem to pop out of nowhere as you continue to take small actions toward your goals. This is going to be a slow-but-steady change, not an overnight transformation.

Four of Cups Reading for Money and Finances

Beware! There may be an opportunity, gift, or message right in front of you that you are missing.

You have so many things to be grateful for in your life. You are surrounded by people who want to help you and opportunities that will require you to grow in the right direction.

Don't do anything rash at this time. This is the time for careful consideration, small steps toward your goals, and constant re-assessment. As you walk this path, you will be assisted through opportunities that seem to "come out of nowhere." You'll know you're on the right path when those opportunities are in alignment with your goals.

Four of Cups Reading for Spiritual Guidance

When you are feeling spiritually apathetic or disconnected, the Four of Cups reminds you that you already have all of the answers you need. You're just not seeing them.

Instead of stewing over what you already know (or think you know), look in new directions.

Explore your spirituality by becoming familiar with the other religions and spiritual traditions of the world. You're not looking to change your own beliefs or "jump ship" to something new. Instead, you will strengthen your beliefs when you compare them to and contrast them with the beliefs of others.

FIVE OF CUPS

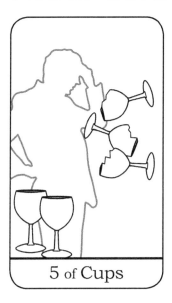

5 of Cups

The Five of Cups is a pretty sad card. It's about loss, regrets, and feeling abandoned. And even more than that, it's about being stuck wallowing in a place where you can't find hope or help.

Traditionally, the Five of Cups tarot card shows a man in a dark black cloak with his back turned to the viewer. He's focused on the three spilled cups in front of him and doesn't notice the two upright and full cups directly behind him.

He seems very melancholy and is obsessively focused on what he lost. He'll never be able to get it back. He's so focused on his grief and loss that he is blind to the opportunities and new start waiting for his attention.

This card arrives when it's time to move on. You need to move through the stages of loss and grief so you can get on with your life. Feel the pain, forgive God, forgive the people you have lost, forgive yourself, and forge a new life.

This card can also indicate deep relationship problems that will result in a separation or the end of a relationship. Some things can't be fixed.

It's actually less painful to accept the reality of your situation and move on than it is to live on the dregs of what someone else can't (or won't) give you.

KEYWORDS FOR THE FIVE OF CUPS TAROT CARD
Loss, betrayal, disappointment
Relationship problems, separation
Needing to work through the stages of grief
A bittersweet marriage or situation

KEYWORDS FOR THE FIVE OF CUPS REVERSED
Forgiveness, moving on
Acceptance, recovery
Hope and happiness return

PATTERNS AND CORRESPONDENCES The Cups suit = rules the emotions
Suit of cards = hearts
Timeline = weeks to months
Number 5 = the turning point
Zodiac sign = Scorpio
Element = Water

FIVE OF CUPS READING FOR LOVE
Sorry. There's nothing good here.

If you are in a relationship that is struggling, there are significant problems that can't be fixed. You've already spent enough time mourning what isn't and what never will be. Instead of more grief, give yourself freedom and move on to something better.

If you are looking for a new relationship partner, you may be caught in the past. You can't move on to find lasting love if you are still fixated on a relationship that didn't last.

Not all relationships are meant to be forever, but all relationships have lessons for us. Once you've learned the lessons from your past relationships, integrate them into your life, put the past behind you, and move on to something better.

FIVE OF CUPS READING FOR WORK

If you are feeling unseen or unheard at your job, speak up. You need to reach out and ask for what you need, as scary as it may seem.

If you are feeling stuck and confused about your career, you may be trying to hold on to dreams and goals that no longer serve you. It takes a lot of courage to admit the dreams you once had no longer feel true. It takes even more to do something about it.

Remember, in the Five of Cups card, he has two full goblets behind him. You have many opportunities as well, so move past your fear and begin exploring the possibilities around you.

FIVE OF CUPS READING FOR HEALTH

Deep loss, depression, and grief take their toll on your body, on your mind, and on your spirit. If you have been feeling the heaviness of despair, it's time to reach out for help.

Take care of yourself and turn back toward the positive things you still have in your life. It is hard to focus when you are in pain, but you have many things to be grateful for. Begin recording your blessings in a Gratitude Journal and search your life for positive new starts.

FIVE OF CUPS READING FOR MONEY AND FINANCES

You may have made some serious money mistakes in the past, but it's time to move past them. Forgive yourself and everyone else involved and start over.

Taking care of your money is actually fairly simple. Spend less than you earn and be a good steward of what you have. That's pretty much it.

In practice, however, we complicate things very quickly when our emotions, conditioning, and ego get involved.

Work the basics, over and over, until you feel confident with them. Work on your money-mindset (the inner work of money) before you start tackling the outer work. And do the "boring bits" like maximizing your employer's 401k match, automatically saving 10% of every paycheck, and keeping to a budget. These strategies are boring, but they work!

FIVE OF CUPS READING FOR SPIRITUAL GUIDANCE

When you are feeling abandoned, unloved, lost, or betrayed, the first place to turn to is your spiritual guide. There is always something bigger than your problems to help guide you to better questions, better answers, and a better attitude.

This could be God, the Universe in general, Source Energy, or your future, wiser self.

Deep within you, you already have a connection to that guide. Take the time to make your relationship stronger, so you will always have that connection to serve you when you feel low.

Start by writing down the things you are grateful for every morning and reviewing your list every night. It's impossible to feel abandoned and separated from your spirit when you feel grateful for everything your guide has provided for you.

SIX OF CUPS

6 of Cups

Traditionally, the Six of Cups tarot card shows two children in a beautiful courtyard, surrounded by six huge cup-like planters filled with flowers. The young boy is giving one of the abundant bouquets to the young girl.

This is the card of nostalgia, happy memories, and reunions with people you haven't seen in awhile. It's also a card associated with the happiness of childhood and golden innocence.

And finally, it's a card that indicates gifts, sensual pleasures (not sexual ones), and fun times shared with others. It's a friendly, playful card reminding you to add more silliness and whimsy into your life.

A happy memory may help you solve or address an issue or problem you are facing. Look toward your past for lessons about the present.

KEYWORDS FOR THE SIX OF CUPS TAROT CARD
Reunion, someone from your past
Nostalgia, good childhood memories
Friendship, gifts, sensual delights
Children, innocence

Keywords for the Six of Cups Reversed
Stuck in the past
Being naive
Unrealistic expectations

Patterns and Correspondences
The Cups suit = rules the emotions
Suit of cards = hearts
Timeline = weeks to months
Number 6 = harmony, hearth and safe harbors
Zodiac sign = Scorpio
Element = Water

Six of Cups Reading for Love
If you are looking for new love, look toward someone from your past. Reconnect with old friends and visit the old haunts. You may find someone "new" among your old friends!

Enlist the help of the people who know you best. Ask your long-time friends and family to introduce you to new people, invite you to social events, and hang out together. You never know who might show up.

And if you are currently in a relationship, you can expect positive feelings of being warm, safe, and surrounded by love. To boost those feelings, surprise your honey with small gifts, affections, and happy memories. Remember why you fell in love in the first place and share your memories and stories with each other.

Six of Cups Reading for Work
If you are struggling with work or your co-workers, start treating your job more playfully. Even in the dullest drudgery, there can be fun. Search for it and share it with others who will enjoy your small jokes, office cookies, and memories of good times.

If you are looking for a new job or career, reach out to your network of professional contacts. Someone from your past will guide you to the perfect new position.

Send thank you notes or gifts to people who have mentored, supported, guided, and befriended you. Show your appreciation and share how you have grown and changed due to their influence.

SIX OF CUPS READING FOR HEALTH

This is a positive card for health, especially if you are looking to have more energy or the playful attitude of children. Return to the activities, sports, and games you loved when you were younger.

If you have children in your life, play with them doing the things they want to do. Yes, it's boring to build a block tower and knock it down 30 times in a row, but these activities are fascinating for kids. Share their joy as they learn new things and explore the world around them. Some of their enthusiasm and wonder will rub off on you!

Although this is a card related to children, it isn't about fertility. The Six of Cups is more about the playful innocence of children than the actual babies.

SIX OF CUPS READING FOR MONEY AND FINANCES

In all ways, the Six of Cups is a positive tarot card, especially when it comes to money and finances. The floral bouquets represent gifts of abundance given freely to people you love and appreciate.

One of the joys of earning money is being able to give it away, but some of the best gifts don't cost anything. Write thank you notes, actually call someone on their birthday (don't just message them), and send little gifts "just because."

It's impossible to improve your financial situation when you are obsessed by your bills, debts, and responsibilities. Too much of your energy goes toward past events and weighs you down.

Instead, focus on the present and all of the things you are grateful for. Train your mind to see all of the good things you have, own, and can share. When you live in abundance and gratitude, it will be impossible for lack and fear to take hold. From this place of positivity, you'll be able to see new opportunities and take exciting steps toward positive change.

Six of Cups Reading for Spiritual Guidance

This card is telling you to take a playful attitude toward your spiritual journey. Searching for meaning doesn't have to be so serious all of the time!

Use the lighthearted and playful energy of the Six of Cups tarot card to guide you toward your favorite people, places, and activities from your past.

To find purpose and meaning for your life, investigate what you loved to do as a child or teenager. Your lifelong interests, combined with your natural talents and learned skills, will guide you to find the place in your world where you can have the most impact.

Seven of Cups

7 of Cups

Traditionally, the Seven of Cups tarot card shows a man contemplating seven strange cups floating in the air. Each cup holds something different. There's a face, a glowing man, a snake, a castle, jewels, a wreath, and a dragon.

The Seven of Cups is about fantasy, illusion, and unquenchable desires. This card shows up when you are living in your daydreams and wishes for the future, believing in your own fantasy in order to escape reality without doing anything to actually change your life.

This card can also mean a bad marriage, sexual abuse, or escaping into addictions.

It's not completely negative, though. It can also indicate a situation where you have too many wonderful choices or where you are in the "creative dreaming" phase of a new project.

KEYWORDS FOR THE SEVEN OF CUPS TAROT CARD
Temptation, fantasies
Wishful thinking
Too many options
Daydreaming, imagination

KEYWORDS FOR THE SEVEN OF CUPS REVERSED
Common sense returns
Things are finally clear
Cold reality ends your dreams

PATTERNS AND CORRESPONDENCES
The Cups suit = rules the emotions
Suit of cards = hearts
Timeline = weeks to months
Number 7 = mystical inner wisdom
Zodiac sign = Scorpio
Element = Water

SEVEN OF CUPS READING FOR LOVE
Be careful what you wish for! This card may mean an embarrassment
of riches, so if you are looking for new love, you may have too many
suitors to choose from. What a wonderful position to be in!

Take your time to get to know each person and explore your relationship
options. Although it may be difficult to juggle so many different dates at
once, you'll learn more about your own desires when you compare and
contrast your suitors at once. Go on lots of dates with lots of different
people to find your true match.

Be careful, though. You could be searching for something that doesn't
exist. There is no ideal mate who will fulfill every wish and dream you've
ever had. Does he really need to be over 6 feet tall? Does she really need
to do yoga every day? It's time to limit your list of desired qualities to
the ones that truly matter.

And if you are currently in a relationship, keep your eyes where they
belong. The grass may look greener, but that's because it's fertilized with

someone else's bullshit. Temptation and unrealistic fantasies won't make your relationship stronger. Use your creativity to bring fantasies and spice back to your existing relationship.

SEVEN OF CUPS READING FOR WORK

Professionally, you have too many options or your head is in the clouds. Take your time to work through each of the choices you have in front of you and seek outside counsel to get different opinions. Be sensible and realistic about your options before taking any big risks.

Use the energy of this card to brainstorm wild and crazy possibilities. These are just ideas. You don't have to act on any of them. But challenge yourself to come up with new ways of viewing, approaching, and solving old problems. When you are radically creative with your ideas, you'll discover opportunities and connections that will result in big leaps forward.

If you're feeling professionally restless, it's because the things you have worked for are no longer satisfying. It's time to move on to new dreams, new goals, and new challenges.

SEVEN OF CUPS READING FOR HEALTH

Be careful how you spend your time and energy. The Seven of Cups indicates a tendency to avoid reality by escaping into addiction or gluttony.

Too much is never enough and it's never satisfying. Focus your time and energy on what feeds and nourishes you. It seems like a contradiction but by limiting your choices, you'll have more freedom.

Stop chasing quick-fix solutions and the shiny new tools. You don't need anything fancy or new to regain your health. Go back to the basics. Eat food where you can identify and pronounce all of the ingredients and move your body every single day. Everything else is a distraction.

SEVEN OF CUPS READING FOR MONEY AND FINANCES

If you have been hoping to win the lottery or marry rich, it is time to face reality. Wishful thinking won't get you any closer to your dreams.

Instead, consider all of the available options in front of you. There are more than you think! Strategically choose only one or two, with great consideration. You need a solid plan to reach your financial goals, not hopes and wishes.

And most importantly, do the basics. If you haven't mastered the natural rules of money (spend less than you earn, build assets, and avoid debt), you can never expect to succeed at your financial goals.

SEVEN OF CUPS READING FOR SPIRITUAL GUIDANCE

Your life is full. Overly full, in fact. But the abundance surrounding you is not as emotionally or spiritually fulfilling as you anticipated.

It's as if you've climbed to the top of the ladder, only to realize it's been leaning against the wrong wall. You'll need to re-define your values, dreams, and goals. Once you are clear on your true calling and service to the world, you'll be able to reach the spiritual and emotional abundance you desire.

But first, stop climbing and get off this ladder. Don't keep moving forward when you know it isn't working. Spend time in solitude and silence, and feel your pain, regret, and fears. Once you have mourned your mistakes (and realized they weren't mistakes at all), you will be able to begin climbing again.

EIGHT OF CUPS

8 of Cups

Traditionally, the Eight of Cups tarot card shows a man walking into the mountains underneath a moonlit sky. He's walking away from the eight cups stacked behind him, leaving everything behind without a second glance.

This feels like a sad and melancholy card, but it's actually quite positive.

The Eight of Cups is about successfully moving on from the past. You haven't learned all of the lessons you need to learn, but you are ready to let go of what isn't working and search for the answers. You've realized it's time to abandon what is no longer working for you and you are willing to look for a new way of doing things.

You don't see the full path in front of you, but the moon (which represents your intuition and inner wisdom) is guiding you toward where you need to go. The message of this card is, "It's time to let go of what isn't working and follow your intuition to find what will."

While this card is usually about a spiritual or creative quest, it's also a positive card for travel in a literal sense.

Keywords for the Eight of Cups Tarot Card

Voluntary abandonment or withdrawal
A loss of interest
Moving on and seeking something better
Travel

Keywords for the Eight of Cups Reversed

Aimless drifting
Come down to earth
Travel problems

Patterns and Correspondences

The Cups suit = rules the emotions
Suit of cards = hearts
Timeline = weeks to months
Number 8 = mastery and prosperity
Zodiac sign = Pisces
Element = Water

Eight of Cups Reading for Love

It's time to follow your true heart. You know whether or not it is time to move on, find someone new, or deepen your existing relationship.

If it is time to move on, you are leaving to open the door for something better. And if you decide to stay, you are leaving behind the old rules and building something stronger.

If you are looking for new love, abandon your usual methods and ideals. What worked for you in the past won't work for you this time. You're a different person and you are looking for a different type of partner.

You have a choice to make. You can stay stuck in the past where you are comfortable and miserable, or you can courageously venture into the unknown future. Happiness isn't guaranteed, but you will only find it when you start looking for it.

Eight of Cups Reading for Work

The Eight of Cups indicates you are on journey to something bigger. This isn't about your job, career, or current projects at work. There is something deeper, more like a calling. You are ready to pursue it.

It's time to follow your heart and desires. Let go of the dreams you thought would be fulfilling but have let you down. Leave behind what you "should" do and eliminate the activities or projects you don't enjoy.

When you get rid of everything that isn't right, you'll create the space to see (and create) what you truly desire in your life. As painful as it is, you must walk away from the good to get to the great.

Eight of Cups Reading for Health

Your way isn't working and you know it.

Our bodies change as we age and what worked in the past won't work forever. Change your routines and habits if you want to stay healthy and see results.

This requires a shift in your thinking. Your mindset must change before your actions will. You must eliminate the excuses and "reasons" you have for not eating well, exercising, or treating your body with respect. You are ready to leave your excuses and bad habits behind.

Eight of Cups Reading for Money and Finances

Financially, what has worked in the past will not work any longer. It's time to abandon your habitual patterns and search for new ways of doing things.

Whether you want to earn more, spend less, or see a greater return on your investments, start by letting go of your limiting beliefs and expectations. Study what has worked for other people and learn from their successes and mistakes. Then walk your own path and experiment to find out what works for you.

Minimize your possessions, complications, and commitments. Let go of what you thought you wanted so you can create a life you love.

This card also indicates travel, so an epic vacation or adventure may be in your future.

EIGHT OF CUPS READING FOR SPIRITUAL GUIDANCE

The Eight of Cups is a spiritual card. The moon indicates a choice must be made using your intuition.

Up until this point, you have been living your life for other people, following the expected social norms of your culture and situation. Some of these norms suit you, but many of them don't.

You are ready to shrug off the expectations of others (and of your past self) to find out who you are today. Your true self will become clear to you when you are no longer burdened by the expectations, labels, and beliefs that don't fit.

Once you have eliminated what doesn't work, you will create a vacuum to draw in what does. This vacuum of time and space will allow you to fill your life with purpose, meaning, and service in a way that feels right to you.

NINE OF CUPS

9 of Cups

Traditionally, the Nine of Cups tarot card shows a jolly man sitting in front of a banquet with nine cups displayed behind him. He's a bit like Santa Claus, relishing the happiness and joy of having more than enough to share with others.

It's about having enough - even a bit more than enough - of all the good things in life. You have emotional resources in reserves.

Your wishes will be fulfilled. The Universe can be very literal, so be careful and clear when making your requests. Love, creativity, security, good health, and happiness are all yours. You have to ask with clarity and decisive intention.

The Nine of Cups can sometimes tilt toward over-indulgence and dissatisfaction. The only way to counter this is to notice and appreciate all of the wonderful things you already have in your life. Sincere gratitude is the antidote to worry and lack.

Keywords for the Nine of Cups Tarot Card
Contentment, satiety, having enough
Material success, good health
Abundance, sensual pleasures
Wishes come true

Keywords for the Nine of Cups Reversed
Greed, over-indulgence
Dissatisfaction
Too much

Patterns and Correspondences The Cups suit = rules
the emotions
Suit of cards = hearts
Timeline = weeks to months
Number 9 = completion, wisdom attained
Zodiac sign = Pisces
Element = Water

Nine of Cups Reading for Love
The Nine of Cups is a positive card for love. You have, or will soon
have, everything you desire.

Be extremely clear and careful about what you wish for, though. The
Universe loves specifics, but has a very literal sense of humor.

If you are looking for a new relationship, focus on what you already
have in your life, not on what you lack. Show appreciation to the
hobbies, friends, and activities you love and throw your energy into
enjoying your current single life. Your energy will draw in a wonderful,
compatible person like a magnet. Be the best version of yourself and
you will easily attract the best partner for you.

If you are in a settled relationship, show appreciation toward your
partner and remind them (and yourself) why they are so wonderful.

Your attention causes whatever you focus on to grow. If you focus on
problems, you'll have more problems. If you pay attention and show

gratitude for the positives in your relationship, you'll have more things to feel good about.

Strengthen and build your relationship by actively appreciating what you love, and honestly and carefully working to compromise together.

NINE OF CUPS READING FOR WORK

The Nice of Cups card indicates material success, but more than that, it indicates fulfillment of your creative desires. You already have everything you need to master this area of your life.

Instead of incremental progress on improving your weaknesses, throw all of your attention toward your strengths and natural talents. What you focus on will grow, so spend time on the projects and activities you truly love. Delegate, eliminate, or delay what you don't enjoy or aren't good at. If that's not possible, learn to enjoy the work you must do. Enjoyment comes from how you do the work, not what you do.

If you must wait tables to pay the bills, then be the best damn server you can be. But when you're not working, completely leave the demands of your job behind. Your job - your real job - is to bring your desires to life with joy. Devote as much pleasure and attention as you can toward the activities, hobbies, and projects that fill you up.

Be proud of what you can do. Be patient with the process and yourself. And be open to every possibility, synchronicity, and unexpected surprise that may come your way.

NINE OF CUPS READING FOR HEALTH

Even when you're feeling awful or are laid up in bed with illness, apathy, or pain, there are still things you can do to change your health for the better. You will always be able to control your own thoughts, beliefs, words, and actions. Start there. Things will soon be changing for the better.

Focus on what you have, not on what you lack. Use your thoughts, beliefs, words, and actions to incrementally improve everything bothering you. The process will start with tiny steps, but they will soon snowball into something much bigger.

Each small step you take is a shout into the Universe about your belief of self-worth. By taking exquisitely good care of yourself, you'll be drawing in people, energy, and actions to help you heal and grow.

NINE OF CUPS READING FOR MONEY AND FINANCES

This card indicates material success is soon yours. You've put in the work and it is time for your hard work to pay you back. The cat has caught the canary. You're feeling smug and sure of your future, knowing you've done everything you can to create the life you desire.

This is a card about contentment, satiety, and security. In all ways, you'll have enough. This doesn't mean you're winning the lottery or doubling your income overnight. But this card indicates you'll be fine. Continue to do the work. Share what you create with others. Promote yourself and your work. Do everything you can to the highest standard you're capable of and continue to push your skills and abilities. And as you are doing everything you can, be absolutely certain of your success. It's guaranteed, so never lose the faith.

Do the work. Do the work well. And let the results come to you on their own timeline.

NINE OF CUPS READING FOR SPIRITUAL GUIDANCE

This is the ultimate "be careful what you wish for" card! When you get everything you thought ever wanted, what happens next? What if you change your mind?

This is a part of your spiritual journey. Like any journey, it's easier to take when you have your material and emotional needs met.

Your first step is to get clarity on your desires. Not the things you think you want, or what you should want, but the specific core desires you need to feel whole and true. Then assess where you are today. How far away are you from accomplishing or acquiring your desires?

The Nine of Cups is a message of support. You absolutely will get everything you desire, once you go for your desires with determination, faith, and persistence. What will be your first step?

TEN OF CUPS

10 of Cups

The Ten of Cups tarot card is the last numbered card of the Cups suit, which rules the emotions. This is the card of complete emotional fulfillment.

Traditionally, this card shows a man, a woman, and two dancing children underneath a rainbow of ten cups. Their arms are stretched toward the sky, appreciating everything they have with joy and wonder.

It's an excellent card for relationships, especially if you are looking for a happy, content, and solid family life, particularly a situation involving marriage and children.

The Ten of Cups also anticipates the celebrations, reunions, and parties tied to happy family events. This includes engagements, weddings, births, family reunions, big birthday parties, and any joyous celebration involving the people you love.

Keywords for the Ten of Cups Card

A happy family and home
Marriage with children
Contentment, "the good life"
Feeling safe and secure
Family reunions, celebrations

Keywords for the Ten of Cups Reversed

Broken marriage
Family arguments and drama
An "empty nest"

Patterns and Correspondences

The Cups suit = rules the emotions
Suit of cards = hearts
Timeline = weeks to months
Number 10 = beginning again with wisdom
Zodiac sign = Pisces
Element = Water

Ten of Cups Reading for Love

This is an extremely positive card for love, if you are looking for the traditional marriage-with-children type of relationship. But even if that isn't your path, the Ten of Cups is the card of family, in whatever way you define it.

You can create your own family. Not everyone deserves to be a part of your inner circle, and a genetic connection doesn't guarantee kindness or love. Only you can decide who is worthy of your trust, loyalty, and support.

But once you've created your family, they will become your biggest cheerleaders, your favorite people, your most fun playmates, and your strongest support system. Your family - whatever way you design it - is at the center of your life and you wouldn't have it any other way.

Ten of Cups Reading for Work

This is an extremely positive card for work, especially if you work in a tight-knit environment where your coworkers feel like family.

The relationships are strong and you feel (or will soon feel) content and fulfilled with your work life.

Look to your next professional challenges in areas involving other people, perhaps through leadership, mentoring, or supporting the work of others.

Grow your professional network by treating people as if they are already friends. Offer support, connections, and resources. Give, give, give and then open your arms to receive.

Ten of Cups Reading for Health

This is a wonderful card for support and inspiration as you improve your health. Your family and friends are eager to help you, so look for creative ways you can accomplish your health goals together. Join a new community of healthy people like Weight Watchers, Al-Anon, or a regular class at your gym and participate regularly. These people will become a part of your new family.

If you are looking to lose weight, get stronger, or heal from an illness, enlist a partner for mutual accountability. You're more likely to get outside for an early morning walk if you know someone is waiting at the corner for you!

Get together with a friend or a few for meal planning, shopping, and food prep each week. Make turning your health around into a party. Share recipes, swap gossip, and keep each other accountable to your goals.

Ten of Cups Reading for Money and Finances

The Ten of Cups is an incredibly positive card, but isn't about winning the lottery or making huge financial decisions.

Instead, imagine you are sitting on a pile of savings, investments, and good decisions from your past. You have more than enough to share with the people you love.

You may not be there yet, but you're on your way. Money isn't the only resource we have that gives us security. Friends, family, and community support also provide a safety net and contribute to our feelings of well-being.

You'll be absolutely fine. No matter the ups and downs of life or the size of your cushion of cash, you'll always have enough.

Turn to your friends and family to learn their secrets and lessons regarding money. They may not be able to provide you with the cash you need, but they have lifetimes of guidance and advice among them.

TEN OF CUPS READING FOR SPIRITUAL GUIDANCE

Spiritual enlightenment and understanding doesn't come in isolation, sitting on top of a mountain alone. You may acquire knowledge alone, but you'll practice it with others.

Understanding how the world works isn't useful if you are unable to take your knowledge and put it into practice.

We practice our spirituality through our interactions with others. Our relationships are the playing field where we learn how to be loving, kind, and open-hearted.

PAGE OF CUPS

Page of Cups

The Page of Cups tarot card is generally a positive card with lessons about love and trusting your own emotions.

Traditionally, the RW-based version of the Page of Cups shows a young man holding a cup in one hand, staring at a fish poking its head over the rim. As ridiculous as it sounds, it looks like they are having a conversation.

Like all court cards, the Page of Cups can represent an actual person in your life. This person is likely to be younger, creative, sweet, fun-loving, and a bit silly.

The Page of Cups card can also represent a role you need to play in your own life, or aspects of your personal development you are ready to focus on. In that situation, this card is telling you to open your heart and learn how to trust your own emotions.

In some cases, this card will carry a message about a romantic proposal, news about a well-loved child, or creative inspiration coming directly from the Universe.

Overall, when you see the Page of Cups, a big lesson or message about love is coming and there are many things for you to learn.

Keywords for the Page of Cups Tarot Card
A studious kid or well-loved child
New love or a romantic proposal
News about love
Volunteer work or service

Keywords for the Page of Cups Card Reversed
A moody daydreamer
A breakup or rejection
Codependency

Patterns and Correspondences
The Cups suit = rules the emotions
Suit of cards = hearts
Timeline = weeks to months
The Page = info and messages to grow new understanding
Element = Water

Page of Cups Reading for Love
This is a wonderful card for love, especially as it relates to messages or new information about love.

The Page is often a messenger, carrying a lesson that needs to be learned. A message about love will be coming over the next few weeks or months, possibly a proposal or news about a baby.

If you are looking for love or are in a relationship that isn't as good as you'd like it to be, this card indicates things will change, but only if you do.

You must become a master of authentic communication and healthy self-security before you will be able to fully participate in a safe and secure relationship.

When meeting new people and dating, focus on being the most authentic and honest version of yourself. Listen to the information they tell you about themselves. Your goal is to learn enough about them (through what they are saying, the questions they are asking, and what isn't being said) so you can decide whether or not they are a good fit for you. Put yourself and your desires first, then decide if they are compatible.

If your relationship is struggling, the only way out of this mess is to go through it. You'll need to ask for, share, and receive information you may not want to hear. Be compassionate and honest. This card is usually a positive omen for love so you may hear news that is much better than you fear. But you must be the one to initiate the conversation to bring this news to light.

PAGE OF CUPS READING FOR WORK

The Page of Cups loves for love's sake. There is no jealousy, control, or possession. In the realms of work and career, can you say the same thing?

Do you work for the work's sake, or do you work for the reward, recognition, and ego-boost?

Look beneath the surface of what you do and, more importantly, why you do it to find the kernel of what you want out of life. It is the start of something bigger.

If you are looking to gain experience in different areas or to pivot in your career, look for opportunities where you can volunteer to be of service to others.

PAGE OF CUPS READING FOR HEALTH

The Cups rules your emotions and the Page is the youthful messenger at the beginning of their lessons.

Take a look at how you handle stressful situations and put your self-care first. You can't take care of others if your own well is dry.

Stress sucks the life and joy out of you, leaving you as a shell of your amazing self. Prioritize your self-care. This is something only you can do and it is mandatory, not optional. This can't be emphasized enough!

Your number one and ONLY focus needs to be on taking care of yourself. Yes, other people need you, but they need you to be healthy, whole, attentive, and present. You won't be there for them until you take care of your own needs.

If you are experiencing physical health problems, don't overlook your emotional support system. Much of this battle for health and healing will happen inside your mind. You'll need to maintain a positive, hopeful attitude with faith. This is not something you can do alone.

Page of Cups Reading for Money and Finances

It is time for you to focus on building your reserves for the future. Although the future seems a long way off, this is the best time to prepare.

Gather the skills, relationships, and resources you need now, before you need them.

Start small, but start now. Today. Even a $5 monthly contribution toward your savings, debt payment, or investments is enough. It won't be $5 forever, but you have to start somewhere. This is as much about faith, practice, and belief as it is about the money. Invest in your future, because your future is going to be incredible, just like you.

Page of Cups Reading for Spiritual Guidance

You are ready to learn the lessons the Universe is sending your way. You can't predict or plan your spiritual journey. Paths are made by walking, and your path will only be visible behind you. You will not be following the paths made by others, but you can use their experiences and information as signposts as you travel.

Information may come from unexpected sources, but don't discount the message because it comes from an unusual messenger. Keep an open mind and an open heart, and look beneath the surface of your experiences.

KNIGHT OF CUPS

Knight of Cups

The Knight of Cups is your Prince (or Princess) Charming, your knight in shining armor, and your ultimate lover. This is the card about romance, desire, and panty-dropping charm.

This is your ultimate romantic hero. Traditionally, this card shows a knight in full armor, sitting solidly on his horse. They are sitting completely still, drawing you in. The Knight of Cups will seduce you toward him. Even if he is pursuing you, it will feel magnetic.

Like all of the court cards, the Knight of Cups tarot card usually represents an actual person in your life. Lucky you!

If not someone in your life, the Knight of Cups could be telling you to step up, romantically speaking. Bring more of this knight's energy into your own life, first by seducing yourself and then by turning that energy toward your heart's desire.

Of course, not all questions are about romantic love and this card can be read in other ways. It can indicate travel over water or approach and arrival to a new situation.

The message is to follow your heart, whether you are falling in love with a person, a project, or an idea. Let yourself tumble all-in, head-over-heels, without fear or expectation.

KEYWORDS FOR THE KNIGHT OF CUPS TAROT CARD
A "knight in shining armor"
Your Prince or Princess Charming
Romance, charm, chivalry
Follow your heart and dreams

KEYWORDS FOR THE KNIGHT OF CUPS CARD REVERSED
Jealousy, deception, manipulation
Unrealistic romantic expectations
Alcohol or drug abuse

PATTERNS AND CORRESPONDENCES
The Cups suit = rules the emotions
Suit of cards = hearts
Timeline = weeks to months
The Knight = learning and testing new wisdom
Element = Water

KNIGHT OF CUPS READING FOR LOVE
This card wants you to have Big Love. More importantly, the Knight of Cups wants you to be vulnerable enough to receive all of the love you deserve, from others and from yourself.

You must open your heart to the big risk. It's terrifying, exciting, and real. Take big chances in love and you will be rewarded.

If you are looking for love, the Knight of Cups will be a charmer who sweeps you off your feet with romance and chivalry. This card knows how to woo you! Don't sit around waiting for your Knight to arrive. You'll have to meet him or her halfway. First, define what your personal "Code of Honor" is. What do you expect from your perfect knight? What standards will you maintain? What things are you willing to compromise, and what will you never compromise?

Once you know your Code, get into the arena. You aren't some helpless princess sitting in a tower waiting to be rescued. You are your own knight and you demand an equal partner. Go hunting for what you desire most.

If you are in a struggling relationship, first look at your Code. What is being violated? What are you violating? You need to address these issues with love, honesty, and compassion.

Your boundaries will be your greatest strength when you treat them with care. Your heart doesn't need to be protected with burning oil, flaming arrows, or thick stone walls. You just need a tall, strong fence with a locked gate and attentive guards. Again, you are your own knight, so watch your domain with care.

KNIGHT OF CUPS READING FOR WORK

Although the Knight of Cups is a romantic charmer, this card isn't only about love. When it comes to your career, job, or your life's calling, you must charge forward to follow your dreams. But before you suit up, get extremely clear on your desires.

Charging into battle without a plan looks courageous, but is actually self-sabotage. Define your desires, admit you want them, and then create your plan of action. The Knight of Cups will support you, but only if you are working toward a worthy goal. Only you can define what is worthy. Your passions are your path. Follow those passions, not the things you are told you should do or want. Be brave and let your desires dictate your direction.

KNIGHT OF CUPS READING FOR HEALTH

The Knight of Cups is an active card. Your body requires regular activity for health, happiness, and connection.

It doesn't need to be extreme. Even a daily walk (perhaps at sunset, walking hand-in-hand with someone you love?) is enough to get your heart pumping. And don't forget those other ways to get the heart pumping, too. (wink wink) Sexual health is just as important as any other aspect of your physical health. It should not be neglected, even if it means taking matters into your own hands.

Loving your body - feeling those muscles move and getting your heart pumping - is both a joy and a responsibility. Love your body the same way you love others. Shower it with attention, gifts, care, and understanding. Your body is you and will be with you every moment for the rest of your days. Treat it like a lover and your body will love you in return.

Knight of Cups Reading for Money and Finances

This card wants you to receive, so keep your mind and your pocketbook open. If you are concerned about finances, the solution is to focus on more of what you want (income, positive cash flow, cash money), not on what you don't.

There are two ways to approach any money problem. Earn more or spend less. You have many opportunities to increase your income. Focus on your opportunities with determination, perseverance, and dedication. When you show single-minded faith in your abilities, your financial situation will improve.

Knight of Cups Reading for Spiritual Guidance

As the saying goes, you must love yourself before you can love anyone else. This is true in a spiritual sense, as well.

In all religions, across all times, the core beliefs are about forgiveness, unconditional love, and a we-are-all-one-ness (with each other and with God). We are born perfect and worthy. If you knew, with absolute faith and certainty, you were born worthy and perfect and nothing has changed that, would your daily actions change? Would you treat yourself differently?

Do you feel the same awe, respect, and all-encompassing love toward yourself that you feel toward your idols, religious figures, and heroes?

Why not? You're just as human (and as perfect and worthy) as they are. They want you to look at yourself the same way they look at you - with endless love, forgiveness, and compassion.

QUEEN OF CUPS

Queen of Cups

The Queen of Cups tarot card is the ruler of your inner emotions. In traditional RW-based decks, the Queen of Cups sits on her throne on the beach, contemplating an ornate goblet in her hand. She is totally focused on what is in front of her. This queen wants you to love completely, without giving up too much of yourself. This isn't a card about self-denial or codependent love.

This card, like all of the court cards, often represents an actual person in your life. This will be someone (male or female) who is deeply loving, sensitive, and compassionate. The Queen of Cups can also represent a role you are ready to play in your own life or a message you need to hear.

If it's time to take on the role of the Queen of Cups, look toward your close relationships and your community activities for inspiration. Model this queen's behavior by setting and maintaining strong personal boundaries before you give your time or energy to other people. If you trust yourself to protect your boundaries, you will have nothing to fear by loving deeply, selflessly, and with joy.

When you are living this Queen's message, you can own your feelings and express yourself freely, while also being a deeply loving and nurturing person.

KEYWORDS FOR THE QUEEN OF CUPS TAROT CARD
An empathic and compassionate person
A mother figure
Help, healing, support
Counseling or therapy

KEYWORDS FOR THE QUEEN OF CUPS CARD REVERSED
Codependency and insecurity
Smothering love
Being clingy and needy, unnecessary drama
A moody and bitchy person

PATTERNS AND CORRESPONDENCES
The Cups suit = rules the emotions
Suit of cards = hearts
Timeline = weeks to months
The Queen = inner wisdom and mastery
Element = Water

QUEEN OF CUPS READING FOR LOVE
The Queen of Cups has the strength to stand for who and what she loves. She is a fierce defender of love itself. When you combine the Queen's compassion, deep self-love, and honesty, you have created integrity of spirit. The Queen of Cups is an attractive force who models an open, gentle heart combined with strong, respectful boundaries. She holds herself to a high standard and expects all others to do the same.

If you are looking for new relationship, the Queen of Cups tarot card indicates a healthy and long-lasting love is headed your way. Someone who represents the Queen of Cups may come into your life (or is already there!) to become your ideal life partner.

This isn't a short-term fling. This will be a relationship that changes your life. This person may have the spirit of an artist, poet, or counselor.

If you are in a current relationship you want to see deepen and grow, it is time for you to step up and take responsibility. A healthy relationship isn't 50-50. You both need to give 100 percent. All of the time. And since you can't control your partner's actions, concentrate entirely on your own effort.

As a partner, be loving and honest with your behavior, words, thoughts, and actions, 100% of the time. Approach each conversation with an open and compassionate heart, 100% of the time. Maintain and defend your own boundaries, 100% of the time. Hold yourself and your partner to high standards, 100% of the time. With each interaction, your relationships will grow stronger, deeper, and more loving. But only if you do the work, 100% of the time.

QUEEN OF CUPS READING FOR WORK

This card, like all of the court cards, often points toward an actual person in your life who influence your world. Professionally, the Queen of Cups may represent a mentor or role model who communicates clearly and with compassion. She (or he) will likely be a leader, manager, or boss with a well-ordered domain.

If not an actual person, this card can also guide you on communicating effectively within your work environment. Even when you have difficult things to say, you can still communicate them with respect. There are times when you must speak up, even if the result might be negative. But to respect yourself and to be compassionate toward others, you must find the inner strength to confidently speak your mind.

When choosing between being liked or being respected, the Queen of Cups will always choose to be respected. The approval of others doesn't concern her. She's only concerned with her own approval and self-respect. When she upholds her beliefs with kindness, certainty, and strength, she knows everything will work out for the best.

QUEEN OF CUPS READING FOR HEALTH

The Queen of Cups is a woman who knows how to take care of herself and others. Can you say the same thing?

And just because you know what to do, are you actually doing it? There is a world of difference between knowledge and action. Learning what to do without taking action is foolish immaturity. Learning and then taking action is fearless wisdom. Which would you rather have?

It is time to put yourself first. You must make sure your own needs are met before you begin to take care of others. There is no negotiating on this. The Queen of Cups is a deeply loving and empathic woman, but she's also as strong as steel. Her strength comes from learning her self-care lessons and taking action on them without compromise.

QUEEN OF CUPS READING FOR MONEY AND FINANCES

It is your responsibility to be rich. As rich as possible. Sitting-on-piles-of-money-like-a-throne rich. Money amplifies your values and beliefs. Having lots of money will make the world a better place by giving you greater impact and influence.

Money is wonderful. If you want to change anything about the world around you, money will be your tool. But you must take care of yourself before you can give to others. Before you begin to tithe or give gifts, you must make sure your present and future needs are met. Once you have mastered your own finances, you will have an abundance of riches to share with others. Concentrate on building your own financial foundation first, then share your bounty.

Trust yourself and respect your need for security. You can be a loving and spiritual person while putting your own needs ahead of other's desires. In fact, it's the only way to have a real impact on the world.

QUEEN OF CUPS READING FOR SPIRITUAL GUIDANCE

The Queen of Cups is the ultimate nurturer. She's best buddies with The Empress and The High Priestess. Together, they rule the realms of unconditional love, abundance, and self-worth. When you need help healing or repairing your spiritual bonds, the Queen of Cups is at your side. Look in your own life, or to the famous (or even fictional) people you respect, for someone who models the Queen's compassion, understanding, and self-respect. This person's support and intuition will counsel you on the lessons you need to learn so you can then teach them to others.

KING OF CUPS

King of Cups

The King of Cups tarot card is the master of loyalty, commitment, and love. He's a great guide and counselor who oversees his domain with kindness, tolerance, and dependability.

He is a calm influence when there is emotional trouble and he loves to support the arts, music, nature, and activities at home.

Traditionally, this card shows the King of Cups sitting on his floating throne, holding a cup in one hand and a scepter in the other. He's the master of the emotional realm and rules with a firm hand while exhibiting kindness, compassion, and commitment to family.

Like all of the court cards, the King of Cups usually stands for an actual person in your life. In this case, it would be a loving and generous person (male or female) who is a wonderful life-partner and parent or who has the potential to be one, given the right circumstances.

This card can also represent a role you are ready to play in your own life. Model the King of Cups' dependability, loyalty, and trust by being dependable, loyal, and trustworthy.

Keywords for the King of Cups Tarot Card
A loving and generous person
A great parent and life-partner
Kindness, trust, forgiveness
Nurtures creative endeavors

Keywords for the King of Cups Reversed
Emotional turbulence or manipulation
Moodiness, volatility
Addiction issues

Patterns and Correspondences
The Cups suit = rules the emotions
Suit of cards = hearts
Timeline = weeks to months
The King = expanding and sharing wisdom
Element = Water

King of Cups Reading for Love
The King of Cups is a great life-partner and parent. If you are looking for a loving and stable relationship with a kind and committed person who will be with you for life, then this card is a fantastic sign. Your King is on his (or her) way.

If you want to have a one-night stand, look elsewhere. The King has mastered his fleeting desires. He only has the time and desire for long-term and committed relationships.

If you are in an existing relationship that is struggling or you want to take deeper, model your behavior on the King's. In every interaction, with everyone in his life, the King of Cups is dependable, loyal, and trustworthy.

Look toward every relationship you have (personal and professional). Are people able to rely on you to be dependable? Fiercely loyal? Honest and open?

When all of your relationships are stable and respectful, those standards will flow into your romantic partnership. You are responsible for making this relationship work. And if it isn't working, you are responsible for deciding on whether you leave or stay. It's all within your power.

King of Cups Reading for Work

If you want to travel the world for business, sell your art internationally, or otherwise conquer the world with your accomplishment, this is an excellent card to see.

The King of Cups is a master of every world he works in. If this card represents an actual person in your life, it's likely to be someone in a (possibly international) leadership role.

If there is no King in your professional world, become the King.

To be the King of Cups, you must act as the King would act. You need to believe what the King believes and think Kingly thoughts. To become the King, you must become the King. You can't think your way into this. You must change your beliefs, your actions, and the way you look at the world.

King of Cups Reading for Health

This card is a positive sign for health. The King of Cups has mastered his own self-care and now has the extra energy to take care of others.

Model yourself after the King of Cups by making your health your Number One Priority. Not second. Not after you take care of others. Not later. Your health must be Number One.

This means your health comes first. Every single day, in every single interaction. When you hold yourself to this high standard, you'll create a body (and a life) that will inspire others. You'll have the energy, strength, and ability to take care of your family. You must take care of yourself first. There are no exceptions to this rule.

KING OF CUPS READING FOR MONEY AND FINANCES

The King of Cups has more than enough money and success to go around. He has mastered his own needs and now has extra money, time, and resources to share with others.

If there is someone in your life who can act as a financial mentor, ask them for advice and guidance. You will need help to become the King of your financial world. You don't need investment tips or complex tax advice. You need an adviser who can help you understand your financial weaknesses and teach you emotional control.

Take action on what you learn and track your progress. You are not alone in this quest, but you are the only one who can do the work.

You must focus on changing your mindset to receive the great abundance the Universe has to offer and never give up on your goals. Your financial health is 100% your responsibility. No one else will do this for you.

KING OF CUPS READING FOR SPIRITUAL GUIDANCE

The King of Cups is able to reach out to others without hesitation or expectation. His center is so strong there is nothing in the world that could shake him.

He has faith in himself. His faith is stronger than belief. It's so well integrated into his being that he is able to offer extreme love, forgiveness, and compassion to others without fear of losing himself.

To continue your spiritual journey, you must first create a foundation of self-trust and certainty. When you know and trust yourself completely, you will walk into the flames without fear.

ACE OF PENTACLES

Ace of Pentacles

In the traditional RW-deck, the Ace of Pentacles tarot card shows a giant hand coming out of the sky, holding a pentacle. This hand coming from the clouds represents the energy of the Universe, sharing its gifts with you.

This card anticipates the beginning of a new financial quest or creative endeavor. It represents the "seed money" you need to grow your future.

The Ace of Pentacles may indicate a new job, a promotion, or a new source of income. It might also point toward a major investment or purchase.

If you are questioning your path, you are in the right place and you have a great idea. Pursue it. Someone will give you the resources you need or you will find yourself in a situation where the resources appear, almost as if they are coming out of thin air.

In practical matters, this card may relate to documents about a business or material issue, or a written manuscript of some sort. If you would like to write a book, this is the time to start.

Keywords for the Ace of Pentacles Tarot Card
A new job or a promotion
A major purchase or investment
A manuscript or document
Material gain, power

Keywords for the Ace of Pentacles Reversed
Get prepared
Gather your resources
Unexpected major expense
Greed, debt or financial stress

Patterns and Correspondences
The Pentacles = rules the material world and money
Suit of cards = diamonds
Timeline = months to years
Number 1 = new beginnings, starting on a journey
Element = Earth

Ace of Pentacles Reading for Love
This is a positive card in all ways. If you are looking for a new relationship, someone will pop into your life who is perfect for you. They will be solid, stable, and exactly what you are looking for.

Take a close look at your current circle of friends, coworkers, and acquaintances. Your new love may be someone unexpected. They may not appear to be a good romantic match, but give them time and the benefit of the doubt. This is a relationship with a slow burn.

If you are in an existing relationship, the Ace of Pentacles indicates the start of a new creative or financial project you can undertake together. If you would like to buy a house, take a vacation, or share a hobby with your partner, start by initiating the conversation about your future goals. Clear communication and a solid foundation of trust will be necessary to make these dreams happen.

Ace of Pentacles Reading for Work

A new job, career path, promotion, or a new source of income is coming your way. Congratulations! This change is a new direction where you will grow and thrive.

You are planting the seeds for success. If you have a new idea for your business or career, pursue it. Start with small steps and take the action steps that will benefit you in the long-term. This project will be a part of your professional life for years to come.

If you are an author, lawyer, or someone who deals with written communication, this is an especially good time to start a new project. Pursue something on the side completely different from anything you've attempted in the past. This will be a project that develops slowly, so take your time and enjoy the process.

Ace of Pentacles Reading for Health

This card is about planting seeds, beginning successful journeys, and gaining resources.

Invest in the tools and professional help you need to make getting healthy easy and fun. Buy a new pair of exercise shoes, join a new gym, or ask a nutritionist for help. Whatever you do, it will be successful, so start immediately and commit to taking daily action toward your goals. Don't delay!

This is an active card. You must do the work. Begin at the beginning and take slow-but-steady steps to build your health and fitness levels.

Change won't happen overnight, but it is guaranteed to happen if you keep taking daily action toward your goals without quitting. Success is 100% within your power and control.

Ace of Pentacles Reading for Money

This is a very auspicious card for money matters. Usually it means money is coming toward you, but it may mean you will be making a big purchase or investment soon.

Either way, this is a positive change. Someone or something will provide the resources you need.

If you want to improve your financial situation, begin small with regular daily actions. Record how much you earn and spend on a daily basis and track where your money comes and goes. Do this without judgment, every day, until you see patterns and connections.

Once you know where your money is going, you can make small tweaks so it will flow into your savings, debt payments, or other investments. The pennies will add up over time, so track and take care of every single one.

ACE OF PENTACLES READING FOR SPIRITUAL GUIDANCE

All gains in the spiritual world are supported by your foundation in the material world. Begin by looking at what you've previously received and show gratitude for what you've already been given.

It's impossible to feel lack when you are counting your blessings. By showing gratitude for what you have, you will be able to attract more of what you desire.

Your spiritual growth is a process, not an event. The journey will take a lifetime (or longer!) and will only be accomplished when you take small regular actions toward your goals.

TWO OF PENTACLES

2 of Pentacles

The Two of Pentacles tarot card is about maintaining balance and keeping all of your balls in the air.

In the traditional RW-based deck, the Two of Pentacles shows a man in a condom hat juggling two pentacles tied together with an infinity band.

This card is either about balancing resources or about making a decision between two things.

Because it's a Pentacle card, those choices usually have to do with money, investing, work, or material matters.

You could be juggling two jobs, multitasking to stay afloat financially, or weighing your options between two major investments. Whatever it is, your efforts are multiplying.

Occasionally, this card also indicates travel or relocation.

Keywords for the Two of Pentacles Tarot Card
Maintaining balance, juggling resources
Time management
Ups and downs
Weighing options, making a choice
Relocation or travel

Keywords for the Two of Pentacles Reversed
Financial disarray
Feeling overwhelmed and being unable to adult
Struggling to stay afloat
Inability to commit to anything

Patterns and Correspondences
The Pentacles = rules the material world and money
Suit of cards = diamonds
Timeline = months to years
Number 2 = balance and pairings
Zodiac sign = Capricorn
Element = Earth

Two of Pentacles Reading for Love
You have two or more different options in front of you. You may be choosing between two partners, multiple relationships, or different paths for your future.

If you are looking for lasting love or a new relationship, you have the information you need to make a choice. You won't be able to move forward until you pick one and take action. Quit playing and make your decision. Both are good choices. To move forward, it's more important to pick one than it is to pick the "right" one.

However, you can continue juggling your suitors or relationships if you enjoy the challenge. Both options have something to offer you at this time.

Whatever your situation, you will have to make a decision and take action on it. You can't keep juggling options, researching possibilities, and stalling your future forever. Keeping your options open will only leave you with options, not commitment.

TWO OF PENTACLES READING FOR WORK

You may be working two jobs or soon have the opportunity to grow your income sources. The ideal situation is if at least one of your paths is a creative or literary endeavor.

How do you balance them both? The key is making choices, good time-management, and communicating your commitments to all parties.

Your side hustle or personal project is as important as your main job. It has the possibility to grow into a new career, but you must give it the time, attention, and patience it requires.

You may be balancing your desire for adventure or travel with your desire for safety and stability. This doesn't have to be an either/or situation. There may be a third option that provides both.

TWO OF PENTACLES READING FOR HEALTH

Your energy level goes up and down. Work with your natural energy cycles to bring balance to your life. Whether you have too much going on, or are struggling between two conflicting demands, it's time to take charge of the situation.

If you have too much on your plate, you have to take something away. You can't keep adding more and expect the plates to keep spinning.

It's time to make some decisions and select the activities, people, and interests that are the most important to you.

Your health (physical, emotional, and mental) must be at the top of the list. If your health is not one of your top priorities, you won't have any energy or ability to help others and it will be impossible for you to accomplish any of your other desires.

Make your choice and turn that decision into concrete daily actions.

Two of Pentacles Reading for Money

The Two of Pentacles is about balancing resources or making a choice. Begin with balancing your resources. You need to diversify your income sources and investments. Putting all of your faith in one investment, job, or project will not provide the security you desire.

And if investing is beyond you, it's time to learn the basics. Your money will multiply if you learn how to make it grow. You must balance today's desires with tomorrow's needs and investing is the way you can take care of both.

If you are weighing your options, don't take too much time to make a choice. While you are busy juggling resources, the good opportunities are slipping away.

Two of Pentacles Reading for Spirituality

This is a very practical card (like all of the Pentacles cards). But there are still spiritual lessons with the Two of Pentacles.

There are many paths and options for you to follow, but you have to choose. What is most important to you? If someone looked at how you spend your time, your money, and your energy on a daily basis, could they tell what is most important to you? In other words, are you actually living your values?

THREE OF PENTACLES

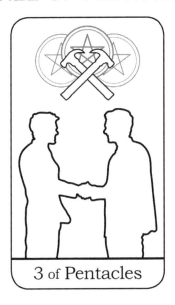

3 of Pentacles

In traditional RW-based decks, the Three of Pentacles tarot card shows a builder carving the details of a beautiful cathedral with two people watching him work. This card is about teamwork, collaboration, and building great things together with others.

It takes practice to learn any skill. This is the time to learn your craft. Your skill and attention to detail will allow you make your own luck and you will become an "overnight success" only after years of dedicated and deliberate practice.

But it's not only about you. No one gets to the top of their game alone. You will be creatively building your career in collaboration with others.

Partner with peers in your industry as well as people outside of your field of focus. By expanding your network and your sources of inspiration, you will grow faster and farther toward your dreams.

This card can be very practical and mundane. You may be building or renovating a house, preparing for a big event, or starting a big DIY project.

Keywords for the Three of Pentacles Tarot Card

Teamwork and collaboration
Skill and craftsmanship
Making your own luck
Building or renovating a house

Keywords for the Three of Pentacles Reversed

Lack of teamwork
Repairing or fixing someone else's shoddy work
Office politics
Sloppy craftsmanship

Patterns and Correspondences

The Pentacles = rules the material world and money
Suit of cards = diamonds
Timeline = months to years
Number 3 = confirming reality
Zodiac sign = Capricorn
Element = Earth

Three of Pentacles Reading for Love

The Three of Pentacles card is the "teamwork and collaboration" card. While it's usually meant in a work-and-business sense, you can also read it as a good relationship pairing.

This isn't the sweep-you-off-your-feet type of love, but it is lasting. You are building something real here.

Every relationship you've had in the past has been practice for the one you'll have next. The lessons and skills you've learned from communicating with previous partners will carry over into your next relationship. You are ready for long-term and committed love.

Occasionally, the Three of Pentacles points to a ceremony, which could be a wedding or baptism.

THREE OF PENTACLES READING FOR WORK

This is an excellent card to see when you have a question about work or your business. It's about skill-building, mastery, collaboration, and eventual success.

Build a name for yourself and learn your craft. Your efforts and talents will be acknowledged and rewarded. People will line up for your services or products. Success is close and guaranteed. You just have to work for it!

But don't try to work alone. Team up with others you trust to build something even bigger and better than you can accomplish with your own efforts.

This collaboration may happen in any direction. It may indicate a mentorship, apprenticeship, collaboration, partnership, or a teaching, hiring, delegating, or learning situation.

THREE OF PENTACLES READING FOR HEALTH

Pay attention to the details in your life when it comes to your health, fitness, and nutrition. If you want to lose weight, get a FitBit and track your steps and calories. The details are important and can be motivating.

Visit the doctor for your regular checkup and have him or her go over everything for you. You must pay attention to the little things and take care of them now. Do the same with your dentist, gynecologist, therapist, nutritionist, physical therapist, or whoever else you trust for health advice. You need to know where you stand.

Once you have a baseline for your current situation, create a plan for small improvements over time. You're not going to get six-pack abs by Friday, but if that's what you desire, you can accomplish it through dedicated action taken over a long period of time. You must do the work and pay the price, but if you do, your success is guaranteed.

Any health improvements or activities will be easier, faster, and more fun if you involve others. Consider team sports, group exercise classes, a walking buddy, a personal trainer or all of these ideas. The more people you enlist, the more support you will have as you work diligently toward your goals.

THREE OF PENTACLES READING FOR MONEY
The money will come once you work for it. This card is about building assets slowly, through consistent and persistent action. You won't win the lottery or receive a windfall that changes your financial future overnight. But you will slowly and steadily create wealth by consistent, responsible action.

Deepen your professional skills and build your network, and you'll easily meet the needs of your customers, clients, or boss. This will ultimately lead to more income.

Practice being responsible with money now, with however much or how little you have. As your income and assets grow, the habits you form today will be well-ingrained and essential to your future success.

THREE OF PENTACLES READING FOR SPIRITUALITY
The Three of Pentacles is a mundane card. But don't forget that the image (in the traditional RW-deck) takes place in a church.

Honing your personal and professional skills is not a selfish act. Those skills, talents, and abilities allow you to serve the world in important ways. Your work matters.

Becoming the best, wisest, and most impactful version of yourself matters, too. The world needs your unique skills, abilities, and vision. By practicing and perfecting your thoughts, your beliefs, and your abilities, you'll become a spiritual tool for healing, change, and growth for yourself and others.

FOUR OF PENTACLES

4 of Pentacles

The Four of Pentacles tarot card is like a toddler - completely self interested, yet absolutely lovable.

Traditionally, this card shows a man wearing a crown, sitting in front of a large town. He holds a pentacle in his hands. Two pentacles are underneath his feet and one is balancing on his head.

When you see this card, you know there are lessons about money and other resources. The Four of Pentacles is about gathering, investing, and sharing what you have. There are two ways to read this card, one with a positive spin and one focused on the negative.

Looking on the bright side, this card is about investing in yourself to create a solid foundation. You are feeling extremely security-conscious. You want to take care of yourself and build a future for the people you love.

On the other side of coin, it's about hoarding and always wanting more. This results in the Four of Pentacles being a greedy miser who takes but never gives. Use the other cards in the tarot spread, the situation, and your question to determine which way to read this card.

Keywords for the Four of Pentacles Tarot Card
Hoarding and greed
Investing in yourself
Desiring long-term security
Fear of change

Keywords for the Four of Pentacles Reversed
Bankruptcy
Poverty-thinking and focus on lack
Don't be such a miser

Patterns and Correspondences
The Pentacles = rules the material world and money
Suit of cards = diamonds
Timeline = months to years
Number 4 = practical foundations
Zodiac sign = Capricorn
Element = Earth

Four of Pentacles Reading for Love
If you have unmet material or emotional needs and you are looking for a partner to fill that hole, you are setting yourself (and them) up for heartache and failure. Until you are able to take care of yourself, you will always be a bottomless pit of emptiness, desperation, and endless taking.

Desperation is always unattractive. It is your job to take care of your own physical and emotional needs. Asking someone else to do the work you need to do to make yourself whole is unfair, selfish, and ineffective. That's not how true-love partnerships are built.

If you are looking for a new relationship, ask yourself if you are the type of person you want to be with. In other words, are you modeling the behaviors, lifestyle, and habits you want your future partner to have? If not, what do you need to change? To attract your ideal partner, you must become someone your ideal partner would be attracted to and want to spend time with.

If you are in an existing relationship, you may be so focused on your own desires that you are blind to what your partner needs. It's natural to want more, but you also have to give. In this case, give more than you think is fair. Love isn't about "fairness."

Focus on the areas you can create intimacy together, through shared experiences, honest communication, and an active sex life. Do not hoard your affections for when they "deserve" it. Sex and intimacy aren't resources you barter and trade so don't be a miser with your attention or your affections.

FOUR OF PENTACLES READING FOR WORK

It's time to invest in yourself. You recognize the value of your own assets and want to see them grow. Spend time and money on learning new skills, investing in better tools, and building the assets to create a strong foundation for the future.

But be careful! In your quest to become better at work, remember it's not only about you. Share what you are learning and support the work of others. You can't hoard the power for yourself.

Reign in your baser instincts. Control and power are assets, but only when used within yourself. Trying to rule over others to increase your own status will backfire and leave you isolated and alone. True power comes from self-discipline, generosity, and confident humility.

FOUR OF PENTACLES READING FOR HEALTH

If you don't change your habits and patterns, nothing in your life will change.

Desiring comfort and security is perfectly normal. It's also perfectly dangerous. You will have to take risks to see change in your life.

You may not have complete control over your health or the way your body looks. But you can completely control what you put into your body and how you use it.

Beware emotional eating and extreme behaviors. If you turn to food to soothe an emotional hurt, you're feeding your pain and the pain will grow.

You don't need to reward yourself with treats. You're not a dog.

Instead, treat yourself (and your body) like the treasure you are. You deserve better, so give yourself the best.

Four of Pentacles Reading for Money

Don't be a greedy miser! Money, like all energy, needs to move. Share what you can with the people who need it and you'll soon see more money coming your way.

Invest in yourself. You are the master of your resources. Investing in education, side projects, fun hobbies, your health, and your community will build a foundation of strong assets. Your health, your talents, and your support system are the most important resources you have. Do not be stingy about investing money or time to grow and maintain them.

Four of Pentacles Reading for Spirituality

Ultimately, the quest for spiritual knowledge and understanding is a search for meaning and connection. Even though we all walk our own path, none of us walk it alone.

As you learn and grow, don't be possessive of your new knowledge. Share what you know. Teaching what you have learned and being a guide for others will help you clarify and cement your understanding. By sharing and giving back, you'll find the meaning and connection you crave.

FIVE OF PENTACLES

5 of Pentacles

This is one of the scariest and most unwanted cards of the deck. No one likes to think about illness, money problems, or being out in the cold without help.

Yet, we all have trying times in our lives. This card is a warning sign to remind us we must prepare for when the tough times come again.

The Five of Pentacles shows a man and a woman in ratty clothes, walking through the snow outside of a church. The man is using crutches and they both appear to be in rough shape. The five pentacles are shown in the stained glass window, which shines in the darkness behind them.

When you see the Five of Pentacles, it's time to build up and protect your reserves, take care of yourself, and ask for help. You don't need to be completely independent and self-sufficient. This is a lesson in trusting good things are available to you, even though you can't see them.

In some cases, this card could also means knee problems or represent someone who takes an official vow of poverty.

KEYWORDS FOR THE FIVE OF PENTACLES TAROT CARD
Money problems, hard times
Ill health
Isolation, insecurity
Job or home loss

KEYWORDS FOR THE FIVE OF PENTACLES REVERSED
Recovery from financial loss
A new job or home
Triumph over trying times

PATTERNS AND CORRESPONDENCES
The Pentacles = rules the material world and money
Suit of cards = diamonds
Timeline = months to years
Number 5 = the turning point
Zodiac sign = Taurus
Element = Earth

FIVE OF PENTACLES READING FOR LOVE
When it comes to love and romance, the Five of Pentacles is not a positive card.

Now is not the time to look for a new partner. You have too many other things on your mind. You must deal with the other areas of your life first. It will be quite some time until you have enough energy to give to a new relationship.

Don't despair, though. You are loved and supported, even if you feel alone. This solitary period will make you stronger, more confident, and more certain of your goals. You will discover the security of knowing who your true friends are. And you'll come out of this cocoon ready to be a compassionate, honest, and extremely appreciative partner.

If you are in a relationship, it may be codependent or one partner may be leaning too hard on the other.

This could also indicate one partner relying financially on the other partner for a time. This is not necessarily a negative situation, as long as both parties are comfortable with the it. Honest communication, trust, and support are key.

This card could also mean marital discord or a romantic breakup.

FIVE OF PENTACLES READING FOR WORK
This card can indicate a job loss or other hard times ahead. If you are feeling alone or under-appreciated in your work, reach out to a mentor and your peers.

You don't need to be completely self-sufficient all of the time. When you are worried about "being left out in the cold" or being left behind, ask for guidance. Learn the power and security of interdependence and connection and you'll be able to trust your safety net will always be there.

One of the easiest, fastest, and most enjoyable ways to build this support network is to offer help to others. Once you identify the people you'd like to connect with, begin to send them clients, information, and opportunities. Sing their praises to others, propose a fun collaboration, and introduce them to your circle of influence. You don't need to ask them for anything. Just give, share, and support their work with sincerity.

FIVE OF PENTACLES READING FOR HEALTH
This is not a great card to see if you are concerned for your health. If you have any worries at all, see a doctor immediately.

And if you are struggling with ill health, remember you can't do it all alone. Isolation, insecurity, and anxieties will not help to make you better. You will need professional support as well as the support of your friends, family, and community.

This will be a slow climb, but each positive step you take toward better health will build on the last. The actions you take may seem insignificant to you, but you are being watched. Someone (who you may never meet or know) is inspired by your commitment, attitude, and perseverance. By taking care of yourself, you are doing more than improving your life.

Five of Pentacles Reading for Money

This is one of the worst cards, financially speaking. It warns of money problems, financial loss, and poverty.

It could also represent a job loss, home loss, domestic disruption of some sort, or a series of bad decisions.

The good news is you have time to prepare for whatever is coming your way. This is not the time for big purchases, investments, or radical changes.

Shore up your finances, insurance, and network of support. By taking action to protect what you have, you'll be able to weather this storm with ease.

You don't need to do this alone, either. Once all shit hits the fan, the situation will continue to decline until you admit the problem and ask for help. You will have to share your secrets, shame, and truth to someone else before you will be able to stop the suck and make real change.

So, prepare for the worst. And when the worst happens, ask for help. If you try to go it alone, you'll make things worse and worse.

Five of Pentacles Reading for Spirituaity

You need help, but the help is there. You just have to ask for it.

Although the Pentacles cards are usually very practical and down-to-earth, the messages of this card are quite spiritual. Do you trust the Universe to provide what you need? Are you trying to control this situation? What would happen if you just let go?

This situation is not something you can learn, do, or change on your own. Ask for help.

SIX OF PENTACLES

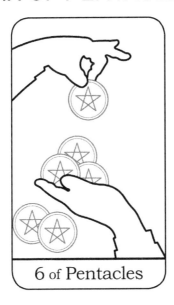

6 of Pentacles

Traditionally, the Six of Pentacles shows a man holding a balance scale in one hand as he gives out alms in the other. Two people are begging at his knees to receive the coins. The six pentacles are arrayed behind his head.

There are three people on this card and they all are important. This card isn't only about the giving of money, but receiving it as well.

On one hand, this card can represent receiving financial success and then sharing your abundance with others.

On the other, it's about being open to taking what is offered and graciously accepting the gifts given to you.

In any exchange, someone gives and someone takes. Both positions are valuable and must be respected.

Rarely, but possibly, this card can also mean rampant spending, living beyond your means, loans, or debt.

KEYWORDS FOR THE SIX OF PENTACLES TAROT CARD

Financial success, gifts, a raise
Generosity, sharing resources
Justice being doled out
Spending, loans, debt

KEYWORDS FOR THE SIX OF PENTACLES REVERSED

Debt
Selfishness, ignoring people in need
One-sided charity, giving with strings attached
Legal or financial underhandedness

PATTERNS AND CORRESPONDENCES

The Pentacles = rules the material world and money
Suit of cards = diamonds
Timeline = months to years
Number 6 = harmony, hearth and safe harbors
Zodiac sign = Taurus
Element = Earth

SIX OF PENTACLES READING FOR LOVE

The Six of Pentacles is not usually a great card when it comes to love and romance.

However, the underlying energy of this card is about giving and receiving in an abundant way. In the right situation, with the right partner, this is absolutely a positive thing.

If you are looking for new love, this is not a good time to be dating or seeking a new partner. Focus on other matters (likely about work or finances) for now.

Get honest with yourself about your role in past relationships. If you have been too much of a push-over (or too controlling), your energy is coming from a place of desperation, insecurity, and need. These qualities will destroy any future relationship you have, so address them now.

If your current relationship is struggling, the Six of Pentacles card may point toward an imbalance. One partner may be giving more to relationship than the other, leading to resentment and withholding. There may even be an underlying sense of superiority and inferiority between the both of you. If your relationship is unbalanced or unhealthy, get help from outside sources. This is a pattern and it won't change until you address the underlying causes.

Six of Pentacles Reading for Work

The Six of Pentacles wants you to share your time, resources, and skills so others can prosper. In doing so, you'll benefit, too. This card can mean financial success, a raise, or a bonus is headed your way.

Beware imbalance in your professional relationships. It's natural to feel inferior to your boss or other big shots, but they're human, too. Treat them like wise and knowledgeable peers.

Likewise, be careful when you interact with co-workers, interns, and students. They may have less experience, but that doesn't make you superior to them in any way. Open yourself up to learning, no matter where the messages come from.

Six of Pentacles Reading for Health

This card is about both giving and receiving. If you are needing help, ask for it. This is not a path you can walk alone.

And if you have extra resources (of time, money, energy, knowledge, etc.), then share what you have with others. You'll both benefit and you'll likely learn something new along the way.

Become the connector who brings together people in a safe and encouraging space to make real changes. Gather a group of friends to attend a weekly Weight Watchers meeting together, start holding "walking meetings" at work, or arrange for a healthy meal-prep night once a month at your house.

The best way to learn something new is to teach it to others. You don't need to be an expert. You only need to be one step ahead.

SIX OF PENTACLES READING FOR MONEY

The Six of Pentacles card can mean financial success, with gifts and money coming your way.

It can also indicate sharing what you have. If you'd like to give to a charitable organization and you can afford to do so, now would be a great time to make a donation. It doesn't have to be a large gift, either. It's better to give $10 every month than $100 all at once, both for you and for the organization.

If you are in financial trouble, you will get the help and money you need, but only if you ask for it. Don't ask from a place of desperation. Create a plan for how you will invest the money and pay it back. Treat all gifts with respect.

And most importantly, beware excess spending, loans, and debt.

SIX OF PENTACLES READING FOR SPIRITUAL GUIDANCE

More generosity leads to greater prosperity. Always. When you give freely for the joy of it, without expectation of anything in return, you will expand your heart and love.

In every relationship, someone gives and someone takes. This includes your relationship with the Universe, God, or whatever spiritual guide you have.

When it comes to those relationships, what have you been giving? What have you been taking? Is this equation in balance?

It is just as spiritual to receive as it is to give. You don't need to be a martyr but you must be aware of the balance.

SEVEN OF PENTACLES

7 of Pentacles

The Seven of Pentacles tarot card can be read positively (as you prepare to harvest the hard work you've sown) or negatively (as you mope and gloom about not seeing results).

This card shows a man leaning on a hoe in a garden. The healthy plant before him seems to be growing seven pentacles among its big leaves, but he looks thoughtful and sad.

On the happy side, it's about seeing rewards for your hard work. The harvest is almost ready to come in. Growth seems slow, but it is steady and you'll soon have the bounty you desire.

Looking at it from the other side, it's about dissatisfaction coming from impatience. You've been working so hard for so long! It seems like there is so little to show for it.

Regardless of the situation, this waiting time is the perfect opportunity to pause, reassess, and reevaluate your efforts.

Keywords for the Seven of Pentacles

Patience
Hard work
Slow and steady progress
Job dissatisfaction

Keywords for the Seven of Pentacles Reversed

Being lazy
Giving up too soon
Expecting something for nothing

Patterns and Correspondences

The Pentacles = rules the material world and money
Suit of cards = diamonds
Timeline = months to years
Number 7 = secure inner wisdom
Zodiac sign = Taurus
Element = Earth

Seven of Pentacles Reading for Love

Occasionally, this card can signify attraction to a coworker. Just saying!

Otherwise, there is no real clear reading for love. This is the "keep waiting" card, so whether you are in a relationship or looking for a new one, be patient. Use this time to reassess and get extremely clear on what you ultimately want in a partner and relationship.

If you are in an existing relationship you want to see grow, keep doing the work. Be patient and enjoy the process of getting to know one another at a deeper level. If things are not moving as quickly as you'd like, focus on building your interests outside of the relationship. Be patient and get your own life.

Seven of Pentacles Reading for Work

The Seven of Pentacles is about doing the work, not about the finished project. This card represents the long, hard slog of any large project. Success will eventually come, but don't focus on the results. Enjoy the process and keep doing the work. It will soon pay off.

The Seven of Pentacles can also represent job dissatisfaction or a sabbatical from work. Before you make any big decisions, reevaluate your goals, desires, and dreams. Be patient in your current position for things to change. It may be time to move on.

SEVEN OF PENTACLES READING FOR HEALTH

If you have been trying to get healthier, it may seem like it's a long slog with slow results. That's because it is! It takes effort, day after day after day after day after day, before you will have any impact on your health at all.

When you are making changes to your health, you may feel the results within days. You'll begin to see changes in your body within weeks and the people closest to you will notice your improved attitude and energy levels. It will take months for others to see the changes in your body, but by then you have created the new habits that will last a lifetime.

Be patient and keep with it. Although it may seem like it's taking forever, you will get there and it will be completely worth it when you do.

SEVEN OF PENTACLES READING FOR MONEY

There might be little return on your current investments or the growth may be slower than you like. Even though you've been working diligently, you're not seeing the immediate results you want.

Before you make big changes, make sure this is not a period of slow-but-steady growth. Delayed success is still success! Use this time to reassess and reevaluate your plans, habits, and goals.

If your plans, habits, and goals are strong and still viable, then keep doing the work. Focus on building confidence, character, and self-respect through this discipline. Taking action when things are going well is easy. Continuing to take action when things are difficult is what will build your future.

SEVEN OF PENTACLES READING FOR SPIRITUALITY

If you are feeling dissatisfied with your current spiritual or religious path, your expectations may be too high.

Doing the inner work to change your beliefs will result in outer changes to your life, but the process is incremental and slow. For most of us, enlightenment doesn't happen overnight in a flash of brilliance. It happens through committing, and re-committing, to doing the work of self-care and service every day.

There is no end goal. Your spiritual journey is about the process of learning, growth, and understanding. The only destination is the afterlife and there is no rush to get there!

EIGHT OF PENTACLES

8 of Pentacles

The Eight of Pentacles is about becoming a master of your craft. When you've found the right profession, sometimes work feels like play. You can get so lost in the flow of what you're doing that hours pass without you realizing it.

You have found your calling and are (or are about to be) happily employed doing work you love.

Keep learning and perfecting your skills. Even though you have reached or on the path to expert status and could rest on your laurels, you'll enjoy your work more if you focus on continued improvement.

Everyone knows you are a master at what you do. You have the history (and the body of work behind you) to prove it.

KEYWORDS FOR THE EIGHT OF PENTACLES CARD
Happy employment
Apprenticeship, education
Creating a major body of work
Mastering your craft

Keywords for the Eight of Pentacles Reversed
Fixing someone else's mistakes
Perfectionism
Lacking ambition or focus

Patterns and Correspondences
The Pentacles = rules the material world and money
Suit of cards = diamonds
Timeline = months to years
Number 8 = mastery and prosperity
Zodiac sign = Virgo
Element = Earth

Eight of Pentacles Reading for Love
The Eight of Pentacles is about work and focused dedication, not romance. If this card appears in a love reading, it usually means it's time to focus on your work and career. So, if you are looking for a new relationship, hold off your search for awhile. Strengthen the other areas of your life so they are solid and under control. You won't be able to enjoy a new romance if you are stressed about money, work, your health, or other relationships.

If you are in an existing relationship, things are no longer easy-breezy. You're well past the infatuation stage and now your relationship is work. Which is perfectly normal, natural, and exactly as things should be. Build the relationship together. Generally (although this may not be true for your specific situation), men want more sex and less fighting, and women want more emotional connection and less advice.

So, if you are a woman and this rings true, tell your partner exactly what "emotional connection" looks like to you. Show your partner how to do it by asking for exactly what you want. And if you are in a relationship with a woman, you'll fight less (and get laid more), if you listen to your partner and don't try to fix their problems for them.

Eight of Pentacles Reading for Work
The Eight of Pentacles is a card focused on Doing The Work. It's about mastering your craft through focused and deliberate practice.

This card isn't about the end result. It's about enjoying the work and the practice of building your skills. You find joy in the process when you aren't concerned with success, rewards, or recognition. Of course, if you are building your skills with joy and deliberate practice, you will ultimately find the success you're looking for. But that's not why you do the work. You do it for the intrinsic rewards.

If you are struggling at maintaining enthusiasm on a project or career path, it helps to ask yourself if you want to do the thing or be the thing.

For example, you might want to play the guitar - but don't want to put in the time and effort to learn it. You want to be someone (musical, creative, and impressive) who rocks out, but you actually don't find pleasure or joy in practicing.

There are other things you feel the opposite about. You might not care if anyone ever calls you a writer (being the thing), but you enjoy writing (doing the thing) so much that you do it every day regardless of the outcome. So ask yourself if your project or career path is about doing or being. Are you doing it for the internal rewards (of joy and pleasure) or for external rewards (of money or recognition)?

EIGHT OF PENTACLES READING FOR HEALTH

The Eight of Pentacles card is positive card for health, if you are willing do to the work.

There will be no quick fixes. This card is not about dieting or overnight changes. It's about a true lifestyle change.

Experiment and practice to find the health path that is right for you. Explore different ways to move your body until you find a few that light you up. Experiment in the kitchen (or with meal delivery) until you find a way of cooking and eating that suits your lifestyle and desires. Don't give up until you find what works for you.

And once you find your path, devote yourself to practicing it with daily action. Measure and track your efforts, not only your results. When you combine focused effort with patience and consistency, you'll see the changes you're looking for.

Eight of Pentacles Reading for Money

When you focus on building your skills and a body of work, money will follow. You must focus on doing the thing (whatever your work is) extremely well, with joy and practice. People are drawn to quality and commitment.

If you are wondering where to invest your money, choose to invest it in yourself. Education, training, and professional development are never wasted.

Invest in professional-quality tools. Identify your strengths and create a plan to improve them. Break each skill down into its basic sub-skills. Create a plan of deliberate practice to improve each sub-skill, one at a time. Join a mastermind, hire a coach, or invest in quality professional training to build the specific skills you need. Identify your weaknesses and set up systems to get past or around them. Hire people to do what you don't do well. Forget about learning skills "just in case" you may need them. Don't fill your head with advice you aren't ready to take action on. Get extremely deliberate and learn skills "just in time," as they become necessary for your growth.

Eight of Pentacles Reading for Spirituality

Your unique skills, interests, and passions are a spiritual gift. It is your responsibility to follow your interests, practice your skills, and hone your abilities. By becoming the best, most focused version of yourself, you will be able to serve the Universe and your community in the way you are meant to.

Our spiritual journeys are a search for meaning and connection. You will find both through service. Your service will be different from everyone else's, because you are different. Your talents, abilities, interests, and desires combine to create a path of service that is uniquely you.

The Universe wants you to be the biggest, strongest, most creative version of yourself. It needs you to grow into the person you were meant to become. Your magnitude is a service to the world and acts as a light and inspiration to others.

Nine of Pentacles

9 of Pentacles

The Nine of Pentacles tarot card brings the lessons of the Pentacles cards almost full circle. You have done all of the hard work, learned nearly all of your money-and-abundance lessons, and are able to enjoy the rewards.

Traditionally, this card shows a beautiful woman standing in her garden of abundance, richly enjoying everything she's earned. Her only companion is the bird perched on her hand. This is the card for individual prosperity and personal luxury.

This isn't the luxury of having a new convertible every year, or living on a yacht without ever having to do another day of work in your life. You aren't resting on your laurels.

Instead, you're enjoying them. True luxury means different things to different people, and this card is about recognizing and honoring what your true definition of luxury is.

There is simplicity and independence in this luxury. You are in your own garden, doing your own thing, and you're enjoying everything you've built yourself.

In addition to luxury, this is a card about abundance, gratitude, self-sufficiency, and the satisfaction of a job well done.

Keywords for the Nine of Pentacles Tarot Card
Material abundance
Financial gain
Luxury
Self-sufficiency and independence

Keywords for the Nine of Pentacles Reversed
Being addicted to work or busyness
Financial setbacks
Envy and comparing yourself to others

Patterns and Correspondences
The Pentacles = rules the material world and money
Suit of cards = diamonds
Timeline = months to years
Number 9 = completion, wisdom attained
Zodiac sign = Virgo
Element = Earth

Nine of Pentacles Reading for Love
This is a very solitary card. When it appears in a love reading, it indicates the timing isn't right for new love.

Even without a partner, you can live your ideal life. Focus on identifying and integrating your values, until you are living the life you dream of. Sharing that life with a partner will be wonderful, but you don't need them to make you whole or happy.

Start by getting clear on what you do and don't want in your ideal life. Identify the values and activities you are willing to compromise and the ones you never will.

Once you know your value system and priorities, create a personal Code of how you will behave. While you are following your own Code, you'll attract a partner who shares your values and beliefs, without having to weed through the muck of jerks and users. Dating will be easy because the "good ones" are drawn to you!

If you are in an existing relationship, get clear on where you end and your partner begins. You are two separate people, with different interests, needs, and desires. It is your responsibility to get your own needs met.

Find an interest that has nothing to do with your partner and pursue it. Build your individuality and create a social life revolving around what you love. Your happiness depends on it.

NINE OF PENTACLES READING FOR WORK

Your hard work is paying off. Keep doing what you are doing, but also take time to celebrate your accomplishments and pat yourself on the back. You've earned this recognition and you deserve your success.

If you are considering starting your own business or pursuing a new career path, the Nine of Pentacles is a good sign. Be prepared for hard work, but you have the strength and abilities to reach your goals.

The Nine of Pentacles represents someone who is secure and confident in their success. Although this is a lonely card, you won't get to this place alone. You must learn to delegate, supervise, and lead others.

Being the boss is a lonely place. To counter this isolation, reach out to others who are at your level or above. They have walked this path and can provide support, encouragement, and advice.

NINE OF PENTACLES READING FOR HEALTH

The Nine of Pentacles is a positive card of abundance and satisfaction.

However, you can only reap the harvest after the seeds have been planted and tended. If you have not been planting the proper seeds of good nutrition, regular exercise, and healthy self-care, you must take action now.

You will only reap what you've sown, so use this card as a reminder to take care of yourself at an extreme level. If you want the security that comes from knowing your body is at its strongest and healthiest, you must do the work.

NINE OF PENTACLES READING FOR MONEY

This is an extremely positive card for financial abundance. Success is here (or coming soon), and it is a reward for all of your hard work.

This card often represents money arriving through "passive" means, like investments, asset growth, royalties, interest payments, rental income, or payments made on work done long ago.

Focus on building your assets as well as building your income. Your net worth is a better indicator of your true wealth than how much you earn. Money comes and goes. The important metric is how much stays.

NINE OF PENTACLES READING FOR SPIRITUALITY

There is true luxury in knowing who you are and what you value. Once you have eliminated everything from your life that is "not you" and "not important," you are left with the few things that truly matter.

The Nine of Pentacles represents the person you will become when you have shrugged off the expectations of others and followed your own path. You will have carved yourself into a pillar of strength and personal meaning. Your values and the actions you take to live your life are in complete alignment.

To become the Nine of Pentacles, let go of what no longer fits. Continue this process of decluttering (physically, mentally, and emotionally) until you are left with the few things that deeply matter to you. Then throw all of your time, energy, and commitment into building and strengthening what remains.

TEN OF PENTACLES

10 of Pentacles

Traditionally, this card shows ten pentacles floating in front of a family scene with an old man petting two dogs. A couple and a child are together in the background.

This is such a fun card, with so many different (but positive) meanings. First, this is the card of absolute personal security. Your life (financially, materially, and emotionally) is secure. You have a happy family and they are well cared for.

Financially, this is often known as the card of inheritance. Your hard work will leave a legacy for others. There are ties through the generations or family tradition, and you have wisely used your resources to take care of your family.

This card may also mean retirement, property transactions, family reunions, the care of pets, or sticking with traditions.

The Ten of Pentacles indicates a solid future with a happy, safe, and secure family in whatever way you define it. That's everyone's goal, isn't it?

Keywords for the Ten of Pentacles Tarot Card
Inheritance
Retirement
Family and job security
Generational ties and traditions

Keywords for the Ten of Pentacles Reversed
Family conflicts or burdens
Financial failure
Loss, loneliness

Patterns and Correspondences
The Pentacles = rules the material world and money
Suit of cards = diamonds
Timeline = months to years
Number 10 = beginning again with wisdom
Zodiac sign = Virgo
Element = Earth

Ten of Pentacles Reading for Love
The Ten of Pentacles is a happy card about family, whatever that means to you. If you are looking for romantic love leading to a long-term relationship, this is a very good card to see in a reading.

If you would like to find a partner, ask your friends and family to set you up with someone who would be a good fit. When dating, show your dates your true self. If you are putting up a facade, they may fall in love with a mask you can't maintain. Instead, bring your best self out and ask yourself if they are right for you.

If you are in an existing relationship, things are going well. Continue to communicate with honesty, respect, and trust. You are building a long-lasting relationship together.

Because this card is so much about having a happy family situation, it can also be read to indicate children or babies. You may be expanding your family soon!

Ten of Pentacles Reading for Work

The Ten of Pentacles card indicates job security or retirement, as well as material and financial success. You are building assets and are able to take care of others.

If you are looking for a raise or to transfer to a new job, you are favored. Continue to work at a high level and ask for advice from your boss or professional mentor. Connect with your social network and community through volunteering and service. Let your leadership skills shine. You will be noticed and appreciated.

Professionally, you are ready to step up into a new level of leadership. You have gone through your apprenticeship and have learned how to do the work and manage others. You are ready to inspire and lead your team.

Ten of Pentacles Reading for Health

You are leaving a legacy with your choices and actions. Others in your family, especially children, are watching how you treat yourself and take care of your own needs.

Every choice you make is a lesson for them. When you treat yourself as if your body is disposable or as if your choices don't matter, they are learning to treat themselves poorly. Be an inspiration and model healthy living through your choices and actions.

If you are trying to lose weight or get healthier, stick with the traditional basics. It will not happen overnight, but you can control what you do today. As long as you focus on today's choices and actions, the future will take care of itself.

Ten of Pentacles Reading for Money

The Ten of Pentacles is an extremely positive card to see in a reading about money. You have wisely used your resources in the past and are now able to reap the rewards.

Your assets and resources have grown into a gift for the next generation. As dreary as it may sound, creating a will and an estate plan is an act of generosity, hope, and commitment. Create a plan today for how your money, property, and assets will be directed once you are gone.

This card can also represent property transactions. If buying, selling, or building a property is in your future, it is a positive experience benefiting everyone involved. Whether you are creating your dream home or building a real estate empire, you are on the right path for designing your ideal future.

Ten of Pentacles Reading for Spiritual Guidance

The Pentacles are very material and practical cards, but they still have lessons for spiritual guidance.

When you are struggling to meet your material needs, it can be difficult to see the spiritual lessons or guidance. But the Obstacle is the Way. You will find the spiritual center you are looking for by investigating, accepting, and trusting the lessons you learn during this struggle.

You are never alone. The energy of the Universe flows through you and can be a source of strength and inspiration when you are afraid, stuck, or overwhelmed. There is always enough and you are always supported as you create your own abundance.

PAGE OF PENTACLES

Page of Pentacles

The Page of Pentacles tarot card shows a young man gazing intently at a pentacle. He's wearing a jaunty hat.

The young man seems obsessed with his coin, holding it aloft for all to see. He's studying it, hoping it will give up its lessons to him. There's more to this card than studying, though. This card, like all of the court cards, often refers to a real person in your life or a role you play.

The Page of Pentacles specifically indicates a young student or someone who studies every angle of a decision before they make their choice.

If that is too specific, then it can be read as a card about research, learning, or industrious effort. It teaches you how to master your skills, talents, and creativity and helps you put your abilities to work.

The Page is someone who searches for more efficient and effective ways of doing things. He sticks to the problem until it is solved and completes every project he begins.

This card could also mean news about money, family, a new job, or pregnancy.

Keywords for the Page of Pentacles Tarot Card
A new job
Changes at work
A student
News about money or family
Research, scholarship, study

Keywords for the Page of Pentacles Reversed
Short-term focus
No follow-through
Problems with school
Problems with investments

Patterns and Correspondences
The Pentacles = rules the material world and money
Suit of cards = diamonds
Timeline = months to years
The Page = info and messages to grow new understanding
Element = Earth

Page of Pentacles Reading for Love
The Page (of any suit) carries a message and in this case the message
could be about a new relationship, baby, or family matters. The Page of
Pentacles represents the start of new responsibilities and commitments.

If you are looking for a new love, keep your eyes out for someone quiet,
studious, and self-reliant. This person may be a bit of a wallflower, but
once you see them, you'll notice how solid and wonderful they are.

If you are in a relationship, this is the time to talk about the future. You
are past the infatuation stage and can clearly see each other's flaws and
strengths. You are ready to take the next step with your partner, turning
your trust and respect into commitment and faith.

Page of Pentacles Reading for Work
The Page of Pentacles card may indicate a raise or promotion at work.
If so, it comes as a result of your hard work and all of the effort you've
put in so far. Congratulations! It's wonderful to be seen and recognized.

If you'd like to advance in your career, concentrate on learning everything about your industry as you can. Put yourself on a course of study to identify what the most successful people in your field do and then model your actions and behavior on their example.

Study your field. Take classes, workshops, and spend time reading and learning from the experts. Find a mentor, coach, or guide who will direct you and hold you accountable to your goals.

Page of Pentacles Reading for Health

The Page of Pentacles looks at all sides of an issue before acting. He or she learns everything they can before making a decision, but doesn't get stuck in study-mode or research.

This isn't learning just to learn. To quote Derek Sivers, "If information was the answer, then we'd all be billionaires with perfect abs."

It isn't about information. It's about what you DO with the information you've learned. The goal is to take action and integrate those changes into your life and lifestyle.

You will make mistakes. You will fail and stumble. The important step is what happens after you fall down. Do you get up, or do you give up and make excuses?

Page of Pentacles Reading for Money

The Page of Pentacles card may carry a message about money or a new job. This is a solid opportunity, but you must learn everything you can before pursuing it. It might not be the right opportunity for you.

The Page does not squander his resources or achievements. He does not rest on what he's accomplished in the past. The Page is always learning, growing, investing, and developing. Make you sure you fully understand all of your financial investments and commitments before you take action on them. It is your responsibility to learn what you can about money, investing, and good financial habits. No one else can do this for you.

Follow the Page's guidance and build your skills, income sources, and assets. Invest in your future through training, skill building, quality tools, and well-thought-out calculated risks. Learn all you can about money and then put those lessons into action.

PAGE OF PENTACLES READING FOR SPIRITUALITY

The Page of Pentacles is constantly learning, growing, and developing himself (or herself). This is someone who knows that "doing the inner work" is actually work. It's not always pleasant or easy.

Set aside time for regular self-reflection and personal development. This may mean doing daily meditation, journaling, reading self-help books, taking long walks, listening to spiritual podcasts, or setting aside time for prayer or service work. Whatever you need to do is what you need to do.

Connecting to your spiritual side isn't something that just happens. You will have to do the work to make it happen.

KNIGHT OF PENTACLES

Knight of Pentacles

The Knight of Pentacles tarot card shows a solidly built knight sitting on top of a solidly built horse. He is holding a pentacle in his hand and there are oak leaves adorning his helmet. The Knight of Pentacles is the least "Prince Charming" of all the Knight court cards. He's a bit plodding and way too solidly focused to offer up much in the way of romance. (Don't forget he's an earthy card, though, so he's got serious physical skills, even if it isn't his focus)!

Like all of the court cards, the Knight of Pentacles can represent an actual person in your life, a role you play (or need to play), or a message you are ready to hear.

If it's an actual person, the card specifically represents someone hard-working who is patient and methodical. This person may love nature and take good care of their body, but probably is uncomfortable with strong emotions. If this card doesn't represent an actual person, the lessons are about teaching yourself (or others) how to work hard and complete projects. This is a "nose to the grindstone" message. It's not very sexy, but it is effective!

Occasionally, this card means a job offer or travel by land.

Keywords for the Knight of Pentacles

A patient and hardworking person
Methodical and efficient action
Patience
Hard work

Keywords for the Knight of Pentacles Reversed

Laziness, boredom
Unemployment
A low-wage job
A stubborn and inflexible person

Patterns and Correspondences

The Pentacles = rules the material world and money
Suit of cards = diamonds
Timeline = months to years
The Knight = learning and testing new wisdom
Element = Earth

Knight of Pentacles Reading for Love

The Knight of Pentacles might not scream romance or desire. In fact, this Knight doesn't scream anything at all.

He calmly looks deep into your eyes and says, "Yes. Yes, I'm the one who will be there for you. You can trust me. We can make this work."

Which, if you're looking for a true partnership, is pretty damn romantic!

If this is the type of relationship you want, look at the hard-working and patient people in your life.

They may not woo you with flowers or poetry, but they are extremely trustworthy and committed. They will make an ideal partner for a long-term relationship.

If you are in an existing relationship, model your behavior on the Knight of Pentacles. Be the steady rock. Don't shy away from hard work, tough conversations, or the truth. The Knight of Pentacles is strong and so are you.

KNIGHT OF PENTACLES READING FOR WORK

The Knight of Pentacles is committed to doing the work. He plants the seeds, tends and maintains them with care, and harvests when the time is right. He knows where to put his energy to reap the rewards.

This is a conservative, methodical, and efficient practice. Nothing will happen quickly. "Overnight success" will happen through years of daily action so practice patience as you enjoy the process and your commitment. Use the lessons from the Knight of Pentacles to craft a discipline for yourself and your career.

In other words: buckle down and get to work. Quit complaining and learn to love the process. Commit to your bigger goals and take it step-by-careful-step until the job is done.

KNIGHT OF PENTACLES READING FOR HEALTH

The Knight of Pentacles is a very physical card. The Knight takes care of his body because he knows it is one of the best tools he has.

This card represents a person (male or female) who eats well, gets regular and enjoyable exercise outside, and doesn't make a fuss about it. This is just the way the Knight is. He does what needs to be done, whether he feels like doing it in the moment or not.

He knows there are no shortcuts. He also knows it's not only about the destination. While it may feel good to have six-pack abs and an enviable marathon time, the real pride comes from knowing he got up every single morning and did the work to make it happen. It's not easy, but the confidence and security you gain when you know you can always trust yourself is worth it.

Knight of Pentacles Reading for Money

This card is conservative, efficient, and methodical. The Knight of Pentacles would never play the lottery because he knows material gain comes from hard work, dedication, and commitment.

Your financial future is entirely within your control. It is your responsibility and no one else will do the work for you.

Today, get honest about your present financial situation. Without shame or blame, look at the mistakes and choices that have brought you here today. Gather your paperwork, open the envelopes, and take a good look at your present truth. Awareness is the first step toward growth.

Your future will change when you do. Learn from your mistakes and your successes. Identify one thing you can change in your beliefs, thoughts, or behaviors. Then create a plan to hold yourself accountable to that change every day.

Knight of Pentacles Reading for Spirituality

This is an extremely practical card. The Knight of Pentacles looks to master the mundane and has no interest in things he can't see, touch, or experience directly.

That doesn't mean he isn't spiritual. It means his spirituality is connected to the physical world.

When the Knight of Pentacles exercises, he's treating his body as a temple. When he creates a budget, he's directing the flow of energy. When he practices a new skill, it's a prayer. Everything he does is connected to the Universal energy through practical, intentional action.

Take the message of the Knight of Pentacles to create your own spiritual practices in your everyday world.

QUEEN OF PENTACLES

Queen of Pentacles

In the RW-tradition, this card shows the Queen sitting on a throne carved with pears and other fruit. She is holding a pentacle in her hands and there's a cute bunny in the corner, but she looks lonely. Her focus is inward.

Like all of the court cards, the Queen of Pentacles may represent an actual person in your life. If not someone else, it may represent a role you are currently playing or are ready to play.

This card specifically represents a nurturing person (male or female) who has a loving, gentle, and wise demeanor.

The Queen of Pentacles is the most 'motherly' of the queen court cards, in the traditional domestic sense. She also has the best garden of all of the queens, where everything is constantly in bloom.

She has created abundance through daily discipline and a healthy approach to life. She loves nature and is a resourceful manager of everything in her domain.

This is a card of domesticity, homesteading, and fertility.

Keywords for the Queen of Pentacles
A nurturing, loving person
Homesteading skills
A generous benefactor

Keywords for the Queen of Pentacles Reversed
Hard financial times
Financial dependence
Greed, envy
Imbalance of family and work

Patterns and Correspondences
The Pentacles = rules the material world and money
Suit of cards = diamonds
Timeline = months to years
The Queen = inner wisdom and mastery
Element = Earth

Queen of Pentacles Reading for Love
The Queen of Pentacles loves love. She especially loves creating a home and filling it with family.

If you are looking for a new relationship or looking to strengthen the relationship you already have, this card is a good sign.

The Queen of Pentacles can represent someone in your life (male or female) who will make an ideal life partner or who has relationship advice for you.

If there is no Queen in your life, become her. Learn to nurture yourself, your friends, your family, and your community through love and service. Start with your own self-care and then expand your focus outward. Draw in love by being the most loving person you know.

Please note: This must be a healthy love. The Queen has no patience for codependency, weak boundaries, or unspoken expectations.

Queen of Pentacles Reading for Work

This card is extremely practical and resourceful. The Queen uses what she has in front of her to get what she wants.

She's created an entire garden through her own focused action. Now that the flowers are blooming and the garden is lush, it looks so easy! But the Queen of Pentacles knows how much time and concentration went into creating such a beautiful body of work. She's proud of her actions and her accomplishments.

If you need advice or help, look for a generous benefactor or mentor who wants to see you succeed. This person will help you nurture your career and guide you along the most prosperous path for you to take.

Queen of Pentacles Reading for Health

The Pentacles are the cards for physical prosperity and the Queen of Pentacles is a master of this abundance.

She is healthy, fertile, and generous. She has a natural approach to life and especially loves the daily disciplines leading to good health.

Model this queen and take daily walks out in nature, eat healthy food grown in a garden, and enjoy your body.

Focus your attention inward to take care of your mental and emotional health as well as your physical body. Put your self-care first.

This means you must take care of your body and health first thing in the morning, first before anyone else, and first in your priorities. When budgeting your finances, put your health first. When allocating your time, put your health first. When making every choice you make, first think of your own (physical, emotional, and mental) needs.

Taking care of yourself first doesn't make you selfish. It makes you wise, energetic, and compassionate. It makes you strong. And you will need that strength to become a loving, nurturing Queen to the people in your life.

Queen of Pentacles Reading for Money

The Queen of Pentacles is a master of abundance and she takes care of all she has created.

This card is about wisely managing your existing resources so you can invest and grow them for the future.

Instead of focusing on quick income, focus on slowly growing your assets to build a solid financial foundation. Small daily actions taken over the course of years will wisely create the bounty you seek.

This is a long-term project. Chasing quick-fixes or overnight success is for foolish dreamers. Be like the Queen and focus entirely on the present moment and what you can do today, right now, to build your financial future and make your dreams come true.

Queen of Pentacles Reading for Spirituality

The Queen of Pentacles, like of the Pentacles cards, is focused on the physical world, not the spiritual one.

But she's living a spiritual life. Her spirituality is focused on the here-and-now, not some heavenly ever after.

For each of us, searching for spiritual understanding is about searching for meaning, connection, and purpose. The Queen of Pentacles has found that meaning, connection, and purpose through nurturing, loving, and serving others.

She has mastered taking care of her own needs and has energy, abundance, and love to spare. She is a pillar of strength, compassion, and faith. She is who we all want to become.

King of Pentacles

King of Pentacles

The King of Pentacles sits solidly on his garden throne. He's the master of material and worldly success and he wants to share his wisdom with you.

Like all of the court cards, this card may indicate an actual person in your life, a role you play (or need to play), or a message you are ready to hear.

The King of Pentacles tarot card specifically represents a man or woman who is the pillar of their community, such as a financial adviser, business leader, doctor, or parental figure.

If not an actual person, this card can represent the qualities of the King of Pentacles: hard work, practicality, generosity, and common sense.

This King is successful in practical and material ways, and he is loving, gentle, and wise. The Pentacles relate to the physical world, including money, material possessions, resources, assets, and the physical body. The King of Pentacles is a prosperous and generous master of them all.

Keywords for the King of Pentacles Tarot Card
A financial adviser or healer
Material success
A solid investment
Generosity

Keywords for the King of Pentacles Reversed
A stubborn and controlling person
Jealousy
A gift with strings attached

Patterns and Correspondences
The Pentacles = rules the material world and money
Suit of cards = diamonds
Timeline = months to years
The King = expanding and sharing wisdom
Element = Earth

King of Pentacles Reading for Love
The King of Pentacles is an excellent partner and parent. He (or she) is calm, loving, relaxed, and generous. The King may keep his emotions deep within, but they are there and they are strong.

If you are looking for a stable relationship with a responsible partner, this is an excellent card for your goals. Look for a King in your own life. This will a leader who appears reserved, self-contained, and wise. Admire their successes and participate in the service activities important to them. This will get you noticed!

If you want something casual and fun, this is not the card for you. The King is far too committed and serious. If this card shows up in a reading, it may time for you to look for a deeper relationship and give up the casual flings. It will be worth it.

If you are in a committed relationship, your partnership is built on a solid foundation of trust, respect, and mutual admiration. Keep strengthening your relationship by committing to a long-term project related to money, health, or the physical world that interests you both.

By showing your commitment to this project, you will be showing your commitment to your relationship.

KING OF PENTACLES READING FOR WORK

The King of Pentacles may represent someone you work with (or for), particularly someone who is in a leadership role.

If there is no obvious person like this in your professional life, it may pertain to the role you need to play.

Professionally, you must become a leader. Pay attention to every detail, use common sense, and do the work you find most challenging. Always take the high road, hold yourself and others to high standards, and maintain strong boundaries as you give energy and time toward helping others.

These leadership qualities will give you the strength of the King of Pentacles and you will become a master of your own prosperity.

KING OF PENTACLES READING FOR HEALTH

The Pentacles are physical and earthy cards. The King of Pentacles is the master of them all. He knows the secret to good health is through common sense choices and daily action.

He is disciplined in how he takes care of his body and is dedicated to all aspects of his health. Nothing stands in the way of his commitment and discipline.

The King of Pentacles is the type of person who wakes at 5:00 in the morning for a swim, every single day. He has reached a place where physical activity, healthy eating, and daily self-care are a regular part of this life. Taking care of his body is an important part of who he is.

If you are struggling with your health, model your activities on the King of Pentacles. At first, you may not want to get up for a swim. But do it anyway. You'll know you have become the King when your long-term goals and commitment outweigh your short-term desires and excuses.

King of Pentacles Reading for Money

This card represents a financially successful person or a wise investment. The King of Pentacles has grown his empire over time and abhors "get rich quick" schemes.

He is the type of man to pick up pennies off the sidewalk and invest 10% of every paycheck. Little details add up and are just as important (if not more important) than the big wins.

The King of Pentacles may represent someone (male or female) in your life who you can turn to for wise financial guidance. Heed their advice and let them mentor you toward success.

If there is no one in your life who represents the King, find your mentors on your bookshelf. Learn about money, good financial habits, and investing from the wise authors who have laid out step-by-step formulas.

King of Pentacles Reading for Spirituality

The King of Pentacles lives a spiritual life here in this world. He is committed to an active spiritual practice he practices every day.

This practice takes place in the physical world. The King of Pentacles meditates about the inevitability of his own death so he can fully live. He knows his time on this Earth in this body is fleeting, so he is committed to fully living and learning while he is here.

Follow the King's guidance and create a daily spiritual practice for yourself. Commit to confronting your fears and excuses so you can live your life as your biggest, best self. Don't let yourself play small.

ACE OF SWORDS

Ace of Swords

The Ace of Swords tarot card cuts through to the truth. Using this sword, you can force a situation to be dealt with quickly.

This is not a card of inner wisdom, research, thought, or inaction. The Ace of Swords helps you take charge of a situation. When you combine new ideas with swift action, you'll see success.

In the traditional RW-deck, the Ace of Swords shows a large hand coming out of the sky holding a large sword. The sword is topped with a crown wrapped in laurel and palm leaves.

Along our journey through the cards, the Aces start the events that occur within each suit. They represent the beginnings of a new path, the spark of something new, or something (or someone) new entering your life.

This card begins the arc of the "logic and reasoning" journey of the Swords. A sword can cut both ways, so the Ace of Swords can indicate the start of a new idea or challenge, or it may mean the start of a conflict or problem.

Keywords for the Ace of Swords Tarot Card
New ideas, mental sharpness
Willpower
The beginning of a conflict
The need for surgery

Keywords for the Ace of Swords Reversed
Stress
Dishonesty
Clouded judgment

Patterns and Correspondences
The Swords = rules the mental and intellectual world
Suit of cards = spades
Timeline = hours to days
Number 1 = new beginnings, starting on a journey
Element = Air

Ace of Swords Reading for Love
This card is a good omen for new romance or any new ideas about love.

If you are looking for a new relationship, take a logical and rational approach. Don't just put on a sexy dress and head to the bar. You might find something, but it won't be what you're looking for.

Make the effort to get clear on exactly the type of partner you want to be with and think through the best way to meet and approach someone with those qualities. If you take the time to think through your ideal relationship before you meet someone, you'll be able to weed out the inappropriate partners when lusty hormones have taken over your brain.

If your relationship is troubled, look for new creative ideas to solve your problems. These problems won't go away on their own. You must take action to address them.

There is a very good chance you are enabling the bad behavior in this relationship. If you are being disrespected, taken for granted, or otherwise feeling unloved, it's because you are allowing it to happen.

Sorry! No one wants to hear that. But you got yourself into this situation and you can get yourself out of it.

It doesn't necessarily mean leaving the relationship. You may need to set (and maintain) stronger boundaries, take more time for yourself, and hold your partner accountable for their own choices.

Ace of Swords Reading for Work

If you have a new idea about how to accomplish your job, this is the time to implement it. This card is about using clarity and focus, combined with action, to create power and success.

If you are in a stagnant situation, you may soon be offered (or need to go after) a new job with more mental challenges. You need to use your brain, imagination, creativity, and personal skills in your professional life. If you are not learning and growing, you will resent your job and the time you spend there.

As this card can show up at the beginning of a conflict, beware any challenges to authority or power. The truth will come out, so be prepared for any fallout.

You could be at either end of this. You could be the one challenging others or you could be the one being challenged. Maintain your own integrity, honesty, and values. You will come out on top if you keep your standards high.

Ace of Swords Reading for Health

The Ace of Swords can often indicate a need for surgery. This may be large or small, but will likely be addressing a new problem or issue.

This is also a card for mental sharpness and clarity, so any health issues may require you to clear your thinking or deal with cognitive problems.

Despite society's stigma, mental health problems are just as valid and important as physical problems. Seek help and address any mental or psychological issues holding you back. They will not go away on their own.

Ace of Swords Reading for Money and Finances

Financially, the Ace of Swords may indicate a new job or challenging opportunity is on its way. This includes creative projects, business ventures, and new ideas for diversifying your income and assets.

This card is about combining mental clarity with action. It's not about knowing what to do. It's about doing it.

If you are struggling financially, get honest with yourself. If you are spending more than you earn, using credit cards but not paying them off every month, ignoring your retirement savings, or otherwise making poor decisions, this is the time to start implementing good financial habits.

Before you can take responsibility for more cash or greater income, you must prove to the Universe you can take care of what you already have.

At first, the steps will be painful and slow. But like compound interest, good financial habits snowball and you will see big results through commitment, perseverance, and intentional action. You can do this!

Ace of Swords Reading for Spiritual Guidance

This is an action-oriented card. You must get clear and honest with yourself and then take action on anything that needs to change.

Spirituality isn't about discovering lofty thoughts or thinking good things. It requires you put those elevated thoughts into action in your day-to-day life.

In other words, it is time to start "walking the talk" of your spiritual life.

TWO OF SWORDS

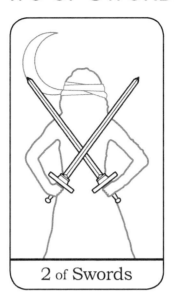

2 of Swords

Traditionally, the Two of Swords tarot card shows a woman balancing two swords (or challenges) while blindfolded (unable to see) under the moon (intuition). Her arms are crossed against her chest as she struggles to hold the swords upright.

She won't be able to keep the swords upright forever. She needs to make a decision.

This card is for when you feel torn between two options or are balancing two opposing forces in your life. A decision needs to be made (and you will likely make the right one), but you may want to compromise or find a different way from your normal choices.

The moon on the card corresponds to the emotions and intuition. Do not rely on logic or your intellect too much. Use your intuition to make the best decision.

This is not the time for bold action. You must go within to find the balance and inner wisdom you need. There is no deadline for this decision, but you will feel relief once it is made.

Keywords for the Two of Swords Tarot Card

Feeling torn between two opposing forces
Blocked emotions
Intuition is required to make this decision
It is time to compromise

Keywords for the Two of Swords Reversed

Too many choices, indecision
Choosing a side
Absolute clarity

Patterns and Correspondences

The Swords = rules the mental and intellectual world
Suit of cards = spades
Timeline = hours to days
Number 2 = balance and pairings
Zodiac sign = Libra
Element = Air

Two of Swords Reading for Love

Are you trying to decide between two suitors? Or between two totally different relationship options? This decision has been weighing on you and needs to be made soon. You will feel so much relief once you make this choice.

All of the Pro vs. Con lists in the world won't help you. This isn't a logical or rational choice. You'll have to use your intuition. If you're being honest with yourself, you already know the answer.

If there has been a lot of strife or fighting in your relationship, focus on restoring harmony and compromises. While you can't change your partner, you can change how you react, respond, and interact. You have a lot of power in this relationship, so it's time to start using it to build the partnership you crave.

Two of Swords Reading for Work

This card shows up in the middle of negotiations or when you are balancing two options. You may be facing a stalemate or truce and want to move forward.

The way through this choice is through compromise. There is a solution that will satisfy everyone. It will require unusual thinking and creativity, but your gut already knows which path to take. Trust your intuition.

Instead of acting on the problems you face at work, go deeper within yourself to see if there are other paths you could take. You may want to change your position or leave the company to find what you seek. Use your intuition and deep wisdom to find an acceptable compromise or result to benefit all parties.

If you have been looking for a new job, you may soon receive two job offers or you may have to choose between your current position and something new. Take your time with this decision. There is no need to rush. Trust your gut feeling. The right choice may not make logical sense, but it will be the right choice for you.

Two of Swords Reading for Health

The Two of Swords can indicate vision problems. It would be smart to get your eyes checked or renew your eyeglass prescription. If you have ever considered LASIK surgery (or similar), it is likely to be a wise investment you won't regret.

If you have been suppressing your emotions or trying to keep the peace between two warring factions, you may be holding that tension in your body. The pressure will not ease until you make a decision, but take care of yourself in the meantime.

Don't rush this decision. There is no deadline. However, you will feel light and free once the choice is made, so it's worthwhile to make the decision sooner rather than later.

Two of Swords Reading for Money and Finances

The Two of Swords tarot card is not about action. It is about balancing two different forces, ideas, or options, and then making the decision to bring things into balance.

If you have a financial choice in front of you, trust your heart as much as your head. You need more space and time to make this decision and are not ready to act on it.

Don't be pressured by outside forces to make a quick decision. If you decide quickly, you will regret it. There is no reason to rush. Just because something looks good on paper doesn't mean it's the right decision for you. Trust your intuition. It will never lead you astray.

Two of Swords Reading for Spiritual Guidance

If you have been trying to control or reign in your emotions and your intuition, stop.

Your emotions and your intuition are the path. They are the way to the solution you seek. Your problems and challenges can only be solved by going within and accessing your higher power.

This higher power is your inner mentor. Everyone has one.

Consider this higher power as the best, wisest, and kindest version of your future self. Go within. What advice does this wise, kind, and knowing Future You have? You already know the answer and you can trust yourself.

THREE OF SWORDS

3 of Swords

The Three of Swords tarot card isn't subtle and it's one of the most upsetting cards in the deck. Traditionally, the image of this card shows a large heart being pierced by three swords, covered in blood, and floating in a thunderstorm.

The Three of Swords is about heartbreak and loss. There's not any way to avoid sorrow in life, unfortunately.

Every relationship has down periods, where quarrels and miscommunication seem to happen more often than joy, adventure, and love.

Most people fear this card because it's seen as the "breakup" card for romantic relationships. This card doesn't always indicate the ending of a relationship, but the down periods will be ruling for awhile.

And although this card is generally negative, there is some comfort in knowing you can and will heal from this and move on.

Keywords for the Three of Swords Tarot Card
Heartbreak, loss, betrayal
Sorrow at its deepest level
Heart problems
The need for surgery

Keywords for the Three of Swords Reversed
Recovery after loss
Physical healing
Reconciliation, apologies

Patterns and Correspondences
The Swords = rules the mental and intellectual world
Suit of cards = spades
Timeline = hours to days
Number 3 = confronting reality
Zodiac sign = Libra
Element = Air

Three of Swords Reading for Love
I'm sorry to say there are no good meanings for this card when it relates to your romantic relationships.

You may be suffering from depression, loss, divorce, or other heartbreak. You must move on from the past before you start to heal.

This is not the time to look for a new relationship. You have too many wounds and unresolved emotions to be a good partner right now. This time is for healing and forgiveness. Anything else is a distraction. Don't avoid the pain. Work through it with patience, compassion, and self-love.

If you are currently in a relationship, you may be fighting and feeling angry, resentful, and unloved. Not all relationships are made to last, so a breakup or betrayal may be the result.

However, this card is not a guarantee for a romantic breakup. If you and your partner are committed to each other, you can work through this trying period. Couples counseling (and individual therapy) is strongly recommended. If you want this relationship to last, you must fight for it.

But whatever happens, you will come out of it stronger and with more clarity about yourself, your needs, and your values. Just because this period is hard doesn't mean it's bad.

THREE OF SWORDS READING FOR WORK

The Three of Swords indicates quarrels, delays, and betrayals. Your professional relationships may suffer. There are strong personalities at play and not everyone is telling the truth.

If you are job-hunting, triple check that your references will be completely positive. If you are looking for a promotion or raise, be aware there may be forces working against you.

Whatever the situation, it is temporary and you will come out stronger for it. Maintain your high standards and don't play petty politics.

THREE OF SWORDS READING FOR HEALTH

This card can indicate heart problems, a miscarriage, or the need for surgery.

Not particularly good news, is it?

You can't predict what will happen in the future. You can only control how you act today. Take care of your body to prevent those traumas and know you will be strong enough to handle whatever comes your way.

The Three of Swords can also indicate more emotional trauma, the kind of pain caused by sorrow at the deepest level. This isn't physical pain directly, but it often results in pain in the body from trying to hold in the sorrow and process the loss.

The only way out of the pain is through it. You will have to feel it and you can't run away from it. But you can (and will) heal from this, so don't be afraid of your feelings.

THREE OF SWORDS READING FOR MONEY

There is no good news here, financially-speaking. The Three of Swords is a card of loss and separation.

Think of the two swords as cutting through your finances, slicing into the heart of your assets and income. If you have built your finances on wishes and dreams, on hope, or on a house of cards, it's all going to fall apart now.

Do not focus on winning the lottery, getting rich, investing in something new, or dreaming about being rescued. Do not ignore your reality. All the lies will soon come out.

To be proactive, focus on protecting what you already have. Get brutally honest with yourself and the people who are affected by your financial situation. Make sure your money is well guarded and you are fully insured for any problems.

This is your problem and only you can fix it.

THREE OF SWORDS READING FOR SPIRITUAL GUIDANCE

Your life has been fairly easy up until this point. All of the problems from your past were reasonable and understandable (even if they were unwanted and horrible).

You do not grow stronger when times are easy. Strength is built when you are challenged. You build your character when you rise to the challenge and thrive despite the obstacles.

This is time when you put your previous lessons into practice. How will you live, love, survive, and even thrive from this point moving forward?

You absolutely are going to get through this. And when you do, you'll look back with gratitude and amazement. This is the period when you are forged into something new. You will become someone stronger, more compassionate, and more human than you've ever been before.

FOUR OF SWORDS

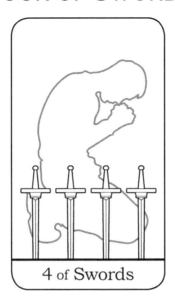

4 of Swords

The Four of Swords is your call to retreat into yourself for rest, meditation, and recovery. This is the card for seclusion and solitude (even more than The Hermit).

The traditional illustration of this card shows a knight "sleeping" on a sarcophagus. Three swords hang on the wall above him and one is next to him. It appears he is dead, but it's best to view him as resting. It's a rest so deep and still it seems like he's dead to the world.

When you are ready to recover from a loss or problem, this card lets you know it is time to retreat and recuperate.

It is your call to focus on a single task, which is the task of planning your next move. When you are ready to move forward, you'll have recovered the energy you need.

Occasionally, this card can indicate a funeral, or a hospital or rehab stay.

Keywords for the Four of Swords Tarot Card
Rest, meditation, solitude
Focus on a single task
Planning your next move
Recovery, convalescence

Keywords for the Four of Swords Reversed
Anxiety, restlessness
Quarantine, involuntary exile
Coming back into the action even stronger

Patterns and Correspondences
The Swords = rules the mental and intellectual world
Suit of cards = spades
Timeline = hours to days
Number 4 = practical foundations
Zodiac sign = Libra
Element = Air

Four of Swords Reading for Love
It is no surprise this card follows the Three of Swords (the card for heartbreak). When you've felt deep loss, you need time to recover and heal.

Retreat from the world for awhile. This is not a good time for dating or whirlwind romances. Looking for a new relationship right now is just avoidance and distraction. You have deeper healing to do and you must do it alone.

Retreat into yourself to explore your family background and patterns. Consider enlisting the help of a therapist or relationship counselor. Once you can come to terms with where you've been, you can finally move on to find the perfect relationship for you.

If you are in a relationship that is struggling, this card is a call to surrender your problems to the Universe. You can't push or force a solution. You don't need to take action or change anything other than your thinking.

So focus on your own self-care, especially on building your inner world. If you have been giving too much, it is time to pull back and claim the time, space, and resources you need to rebuild your life and sense of self.

FOUR OF SWORDS READING FOR WORK

The Four of Swords is not about work at all. It's about not working!

This card shows up after you've made a huge push to meet your deadlines and are exhausted. It arrives when you've experienced an unexpected loss or when you need a break.

But this break isn't for family vacations and fun. This break must be a sabbatical of rest and recuperation. This card indicates it is time for you to retreat into yourself, so you can rest and plan your next move.

If you are nearing the end of your professional career, this card can indicate retirement in the official sense, as well.

FOUR OF SWORDS READING FOR HEALTH

This card is about convalescence and recovery. If you've been facing health problems, you must take the time to heal and recuperate.

The recovery may take longer than you'd like, but it is absolutely necessary. This is a perfect time to focus on you. Use this time to create the habits and routines to help you live a healthy life from this point on.

This card can also indicate a hospital stay or rehab. It's a necessary break from the world for healing and growth.

FOUR OF SWORDS READING FOR MONEY

If you have financial problems such as debt, unexpected bills, tax issues, uninsured losses, or other money issues, this is the time to begin your recovery.

There is nothing grand or quick about the recovery process. Just like you would need time to recover from a heartbreak or surgery, you'll need time to recover from this as well.

Begin by objectively looking at your financial situation with honesty and without judgment. These are numbers and facts. They don't represent your worth or your abilities or your value. But you need to know the truth.

Once you know where you stand, begin learning about money and how to improve your financial future. When you are ready, take a look at these two books: Your Money or Your Life and Total Money Makeover. They will give you a new way of looking at your situation and provide a solid plan for creating good financial habits.

The road to financial recovery and responsibility will be slow, especially at first. But it will take much less time than you fear. Get started today.

Four of Swords Reading for Spiritual Guidance

The Four of Swords is about your inner journey. It is easy to lose yourself in the day-to-day, where ego takes hold. But you can't stay stuck any longer.

You need to break away to find yourself, your voice, and your deep inner wisdom.

This doesn't have to be a month-long retreat to a cabin in the woods (although that's a wonderful idea if you can do it).

Small daily actions, like meditating, journaling, or a media fast will give you the time and mental space to retreat from the world.

FIVE OF SWORDS

5 of Swords

The Five of Swords shows someone (you?) spoiling for a fight. You're in the war zone and this conflict can't be avoided.

Unfortunately, this conflict is likely to be unequal, unfair, or abusive. You do have a choice, though. You can fight this unfair fight or you can learn from the situation, grow, and move on.

Of course, the better option is to learn from this situation. Fighting this battle will likely end in defeat. Even if you do somehow come out on top, the victory will be hollow and you'll lose much more than you hoped to gain.

Traditionally, this card shows a mean-looking man holding three swords, with two at his feet. He's looking over his shoulder at two defeated men walking away. There's something about his face that makes this guy look like a jerk.

The jerk might be someone in your life, or it might be YOU. If you find yourself playing the role of the bully, stop. There is a deeper fear or desire driving you. Deal with that deeper issue instead of taking your pain out on the people around you.

KEYWORDS FOR THE FIVE OF SWORDS TAROT CARD
War, violence, bullies
Victory through deceit, poor sportsmanship
Betrayal, loss, defeat
Failed relationships

KEYWORDS FOR THE FIVE OF SWORDS REVERSED
A fair fight
Peace after a violent act
Moving past resentments
The lies come out

PATTERNS AND CORRESPONDENCES
The Swords = rules the mental and intellectual world
Suit of cards = spades
Timeline = hours to days
Number 5 = the turning point
Zodiac sign = Aquarius
Element = Air

FIVE OF SWORDS READING FOR LOVE
This is not a good card for love and it may indicate an abusive relationship.

Not every relationship is meant to last, but they are all meant to teach us something. What have you learned from your current and past relationships? Are you ready to move on?

If you are in a rocky relationship, be honest with yourself. Your words, choices, and actions are contributing to the situation. You are as much responsible for allowing and enabling this bad behavior as your partner is.

You wouldn't tolerate this bad behavior from your best friend, boss, or a stranger. Don't stay in an unhappy situation unless you both are doing the work to make it better. You deserve so much more than this.

If you are looking for a new relationship, beware situations where there is an obvious power difference. This could be age, money, or status. Overall, I'd say now is NOT a good time for love, so be careful if you go hunting for it.

Five of Swords Reading for Work

In a practical and material sense, this card can indicate office politics, dirty tricks in the workplace, or a hostile takeover of your company.

Watch your back. Keep your secrets close. Even people who seem trustworthy may betray your confidences. They have their own worries, problems, and fears. You are not their priority. Protect yourself and keep your standards high.

If you have been playing dirty and trying to win at all costs, this will soon come back to bite you. Reassess your strategy and motivations. You will not win through deceit or manipulation. That's a game you don't want to play.

Five of Swords Reading for Health

The Five of Swords tarot card indicates a conflict, tension, loss, or betrayal.

If you are trying to get healthy or are facing a health problem, don't take shortcuts or try to cheat. It won't work and you'll make things worse in the long run.

There are no pills, diets, or trendy exercise machines that will solve your problems. Stick with the basics and don't expect overnight success. The process can actually be as enjoyable as the results, if you make it so!

You may be suffering from abuse. This may be abuse from someone else, or from yourself. If you have been abusing your body, it is coming to a head. You can't continue punishing yourself in this way. It is time to get help.

Five of Swords Reading for Money and Finances

This card indicates theft, betrayal, and deceit. Not good when it comes to financial decisions.

Right now, don't trust anyone to manage your money for you and don't make large investments until you completely understand them. This means completely.

If you are concerned about someone else's behavior, you should be. There is something going on behind the scenes and it isn't in your favor.

Don't be a bully with your money, either. Using money to manipulate or control the behaviors of others is abusive. There are far easier (and more compassionate) ways to get your needs met.

Five of Swords Reading for Spiritual Guidance

This card is a reminder to look deep within at your own negative behaviors. We all have our ego-led shadow side. We all do stupid stuff, make terrible mistakes, and have deep regrets.

These dark, shadowy behaviors and choices are a part of being human. If you continue to ignore, overlook, or hide them, you will never grow into the fully-realized person you are meant to become.

Start by forgiving yourself. You did the absolute best you could at the time.

Until you embrace and accept your negative qualities and reactions, you'll never be able to fully accept your whole self. You need the dark to give definition to the light.

SIX OF SWORDS

6 of Swords

The Six of Swords tarot card is about acceptance and moving on from the past. It's the card of starting over.

Traditionally, this card shows a man ferrying a woman and child across a river to their new life. They don't want to leave, but they must. They are leaving behind a painful situation to start over.

They have accepted the reality of their situation and their backs are turned on the past. They are facing their destiny while hopeful for the future.

When you are ready to leave your sorrows behind and start a new life, the Six of Swords is the card for you. You must look at things as they actually are, not as you wish them to be. Accept the reality of the situation, no matter how painful it is to admit the truth. Move on and don't look back.

Once you accept the reality of your situation and move on, the struggle will be over. The pain will be in your past. You are ready for something new, even though you don't know what the future holds.

This a very hopeful card. Once you take action to move toward your new future, you will have smooth sailing and things will change with ease.

In some cases, this card may indicate a literal move or relocation, or a short trip or vacation. If that's the case, you will likely travel over water.

KEYWORDS FOR THE SIX OF SWORDS TAROT CARD
Moving to a safer environment
Leaving the past behind and starting over
A regretful but necessary rite of passage
Travel (over water), relocating

KEYWORDS FOR THE SIX OF SWORDS REVERSED
You're stuck and can't move on
Someone is holding you back
Fear of travel or travel problems

PATTERNS AND CORRESPONDENCES
The Swords = rules the mental and intellectual world
Suit of cards = spades
Timeline = hours to days
Number 6 = harmony, hearth and safe harbors
Zodiac sign = Aquarius
Element = Air

SIX OF SWORDS READING FOR LOVE
In a love reading, the Six of Swords usually indicates moving on from heartbreak.

To move on, you will must leave your anxieties behind and jump into the unknown. But things get much better from here, so don't be afraid of the leap.

If you are looking for new love, you must make a clean break from your past. Your future is much brighter than anything you can currently imagine. Let the past go so you can welcome this new future into your life.

If you are in a committed relationship, you still must let the past go. Forgive yourself and your partner and make a new start together. You have the opportunity to build something better and stronger, but you must let the past stay in the past, for good.

SIX OF SWORDS READING FOR WORK

This card indicates a regretful but necessary transition, such as being laid off or losing an important client. However, this is for the best, as it opens you up for something even better.

While this situation may feel crushing, it is not a permanent blow. You have so many options now. Ask for advice from someone outside your field and focus your attention on the positive changes and opportunities you now have.

If you're feeling stuck in your career or work, it may be time to find another way to reach your goals. There will be a big leap ahead, but you will be ready for it. Find the work that interests you (in your current job or elsewhere) and throw yourself into it.

Most adults have multiple careers during their lives. (Not just multiple jobs, but multiple different career paths). Your future might be radically different from your past or the present. To find this new direction, begin by removing everything that doesn't fit. As you eliminate the things that don't fit, you will create a vacuum of space and energy to attract what is truly you.

SIX OF SWORDS READING FOR HEALTH

You must look at things as they are, not as you want them to be. Once you see clearly, the struggle will be over and you will be able to commit to your next step.

This is a hopeful card. Although the past has been awful and the current situation isn't ideal, this is the turning point toward something better.

But you must take action. You can't sit around waiting for things to change. You must make a commitment to your future by doing the one thing you fear the most.

Six of Swords Reading for Money and Finances
The Six of Swords card can indicate a relocation, move, or short vacation - all of which cost money.

If you have made stupid financial decisions in the past, forgive yourself and accept your current situation as it is. There is no point in wishing for the past to be different. While you can't change the past, you can change your present situation and the future.

It is time to take specific actions to make your financial life better. This means growing up and taking responsibility for every financial decision you make.

The pennies count. If you treat them with respect, the dollars will take care of themselves.

Six of Swords Reading for Spiritual Guidance
Step back to gain perspective on your problems. There are many things you don't see and will never understand about the events in your life and how they affect you. As humans, our knowledge is limited by our own experiences and what we learn by observing others.

No matter how hard we try, we will never fully understand or know the people in our lives. They have their own secrets, desires, wounds, and motivations. And their actions will impact your life, in both good and bad ways.

You must learn to separate yourself from other people and trust your own wisdom. You must forgive them and yourself. And you must leave behind your sorrows, disappointments, and unfulfilled hopes before you can create the life you desire.

SEVEN OF SWORDS

7 of Swords

The Seven of Swords tarot card is about betrayal through trickery and dishonesty. Someone is being sneaky and is lying to you.

This card has a strong association with illicit affairs or divorce. This isn't a guarantee, but it is a warning.

Traditionally, the Seven of Swords shows a man stealing five swords, with two in the ground behind him. He's looking backward over his shoulder as he tip-toes away.

In a modern sense, this card also points indicates gossip, spreading rumors or lies, or criminal behavior.

When you have someone gossiping about you, copying you, or hating on you in some way, it's rooted in jealousy. As much as their words and behaviors hurt, their judgmental and critical behavior actually says more about their wounds than it does about your choices.

It's cold comfort, but it may help you take the high road.

Many people mix up the Five of Swords with this card. They both have jerks doing stupid stuff with swords. Where the Five of Swords is about violence and betrayal, this card is about dishonesty and criminal activity. This card can also meaning running away or giving up after half-assed effort.

The Seven of Swords doesn't necessarily point toward other people. You may be the jerk who is gossiping, lying, or stealing. If that's the case, be prepared to have the truth come to light quickly. You will have to pay for the pain you've caused.

KEYWORDS FOR THE SEVEN OF SWORDS TAROT CARD
Trickery, betrayal, lies
Theft, criminal activity
Cutting corners or barely trying
Running away

KEYWORDS FOR THE SEVEN OF SWORDS REVERSED
The truth is revealed
Getting caught, punishment
Trying to make things right

PATTERNS AND CORRESPONDENCES
The Swords = rules the mental and intellectual world
Suit of cards = spades
Timeline = hours to days
Number 7 = accepting inner wisdom
Zodiac sign = Aquarius
Element = Air

SEVEN OF SWORDS READING FOR LOVE
There are no positive associations with love and the Seven of Swords. In a love reading, at least one of the partners is being dishonest and may be cheating.

If you are looking for a new relationship, protect yourself. At least one of the people you are dating is not being honest with you.

On the flip side, you may be the one who is dishonest. It's natural to want to present your best self when dating, but don't become fake or wear a mask that doesn't represent who you are. You'll never be able to maintain it and you'll be pushing away the people who actually are right for you.

If you are in an existing relationship, commit to doing the work of staying connected. While you can't control your partner's behavior, you can control how much you prioritize the relationship. Focus on building the togetherness through fun, love, sexy-times, and unconditional support.

If they do stray, it's their problem. You don't need to tolerate it or claim ownership for their behavior.

SEVEN OF SWORDS READING FOR WORK

Someone is telling lies and is manipulating the situation to get ahead. They could be sabotaging your efforts behind your back. Office politics are definitely at play.

If you have jealous copycats, haters, or thieves taking credit for your work, set and enforce strong boundaries. This could go as far as hiring a lawyer to protect what is yours. When it comes to your livelihood, it's worth it.

This card could also be about your own behavior. If you've been acting in an underhanded manner, shape up before you are found out. And you will be found out, likely very soon. The pain you'll suffer is not worth what you are gaining now.

SEVEN OF SWORDS READING FOR HEALTH

If you have been going half-assed on your health, this is the time to shape up. You won't see improvement until you make those improvements happen.

Your unstable effort is only making things worse. There are no shortcuts or easy fixes. If your health hasn't improved in the last year (or last five years!) it's because you haven't made it a priority.

Make this year the year you change. Commit to the long haul and do the work without cheating, looking for quick-fixes, or taking short-cuts. You can't ignore your problems any longer. The truth will quickly come out.

SEVEN OF SWORDS READING FOR MONEY

Beware someone taking your money, belongings, or other resources.

Make sure everything is fully insured and secured. Check your locks and security system. Hide what you don't want found.

This is not the time for big investments. People can be shady, especially when money is involved. It's so hard to know who to trust and it's likely you don't have all the information you need. Take your time with this decision and if it doesn't feel right in your gut, walk away.

If you've been borrowing money, beware. You're about to tip too far into debt and may not be able to crawl out of the hole. This situation is not sustainable and you've been lying about it for too long.

Take responsibility for your past actions, your current financial reality, and your future goals. It will be a slow climb back to financial wellness, but you can do it.

SEVEN OF SWORDS READING FOR SPIRITUAL GUIDANCE

This card does not have a strong spiritual message. Instead, it's about being aware of the negative aspects of the mundane world around us.

Not everyone is a nice person. People are sometimes dishonest. This includes religious leaders, spiritual gurus, and even ourselves.

If something doesn't feel right, it isn't. Walk away from any situation that goes against your values. Standing up for yourself and what you know is right is a spiritual act.

It's only when you can fully accept your darkest flaws and all of the times you have hurt others that you'll be able to accept yourself. This acceptance of your "shadow side" is a requirement for spiritual awakening and unconditional self-love.

EIGHT OF SWORDS

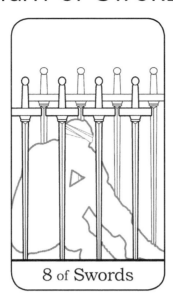

8 of Swords

The Eight of Swords tarot card is about feeling trapped and helpless. When you are immobilized by fear, you must feel the fear as you take action anyway.

In the traditional RW-based deck, the Eight of Swords card shows a blindfolded and bound woman standing on a beach in the middle of eight swords. She's fenced in with nowhere to turn. She feels as if every choice or step forward will result in pain and she is blind to any other options.

This card has two interpretations, both related to feeling trapped. You are either trapped by fear or by your own unhelpful actions.

Either way, you are in a self-imposed prison. You have been stuck, looping repetitive behaviors without learning the lessons you need to learn.

While there may be some interference from outside forces, it is likely all of your current problems are self-imposed.

You have been hijacked by your limiting beliefs. Although the beliefs feel real, they are holding you back. The only way to get out of this situation is to take off your blindfold and see the reality of the situation. What you believe is not true. You must change your beliefs, which will allow you to change your thoughts, words, actions, and choices. Change must happen from the inside first.

Occasionally, this card indicates legal problems or actual imprisonment.

Keywords for the Eight of Swords Tarot Card
Self-imposed limitations
Imprisonment, isolation
Feeling immobilized by fear
Interference by outside forces

Keywords for the Eight of Swords Reversed
Release, liberation
Escape, freedom
Seeing beyond your fears

Patterns and Correspondences
The Swords = rules the mental and intellectual world
Suit of cards = spades
Timeline = hours to days
Number 8 = mastery and prosperity
Zodiac sign = Gemini
Element = Air

Eight of Swords Reading for Love
The Eight of Swords is not a good card to see in a love reading. If you are looking for new love, you are too tied to your expectations and fears. You can't expect to control everything - especially not who you fall in love with! Your list of requirements for your future partner is too stringent. And let's face it - you aren't living up to those standards, so why are you expecting someone else to?

(And even if you did find this 'perfect' partner, would they consider you their equal if you aren't living up to your own standards? Ouch. The truth hurts, doesn't it?)

If you are in a relationship, you may feel trapped. The only way to get through this rough patch is to honestly communicate your feelings and to respond to what is actually being said (not what you hope, expect, or fear).

You'll need to change something for things to change. Start with changing the things you can control immediately, such as your thoughts, the words you say, and the choices you make.

EIGHT OF SWORDS READING FOR WORK

If you are feeling trapped in a job you do not enjoy, all of your limitations are self-imposed. You have many more options than you think.

To begin to see these possibilities, create a list of 10 alternate ways you could make money. Repeat this brainstorming list for 10 days. Do not limit yourself to "sensible" or "realistic" choices. Not only will you come up with many options for a new career, but you will have jump-started your creativity and opened your eyes to new ideas.

Study other people who have made radical life changes. Ask your personal and professional network if they know anyone who has followed the career path you are curious about, and then invite that person out for coffee or ask them for advice. You don't have to make a choice or a change yet. But you must realize you have options and the best way to do it is through creativity, imagination, curiosity, and following the paths shown by others.

EIGHT OF SWORDS READING FOR HEALTH

Things will only change once you do. If you are feeling like your body has betrayed you due to illness or age, you will only be able to get past these limiting beliefs once you change your attitude.

To move forward, get past your fears and feelings of helplessness. The only thing holding you back is your self-imposed sense of reality. You don't need to be a victim of your past choices.

Begin by thinking, "What if…?" in a positive way. For example, what if changing your diet was easy? What if your friends and family were 100%

supportive? What if exercising gave you more energy? What if someone wanted to help you?

You'll find that everything changes when you begin looking at things from a different, more positive perspective and believe change is possible.

Eight of Swords Reading for Money

One of the most common self-imposed limiting beliefs is the idea, "I can't to this thing until I have more money." Another way of phrasing this is, "Once I have more money (or time), I'll be able to follow my dreams."

What if that belief wasn't true? The lack of money isn't holding you back. It's your beliefs keeping you stuck. There are dozens, if not hundreds, ways for you to accomplish each of your desires. Only one of them involves trading money to get what you want. Be creative and come up with 10 (or 100!) alternative ways to accomplish your dream without using money. You'll soon see you have many options. You are being limited by your excuses and negative thinking, not your actual financial situation.

Eight of Swords Reading for Spiritual Guidance

Right now, you are too wrapped in the material world of wishing and wanting things to be different. Until you change your attitudes about what is holding you back, you won't ever be able to connect with your spiritual side. Your negative beliefs are limiting your life. The Universe is unlimited and infinite. This disconnect between your ego's striving and the Universe's abundance is keeping you locked in a prison of your own making. Let the Universe do its job. It wants you to thrive, succeed, and be the best version of yourself. The Universe is also infinitely smarter than you are. Quit trying to force your small vision and let the Big U take over.

Surrender all your striving, control, and pushing. Ask the Universe (or God or whoever you trust) to give you the wisdom, strength, and compassion you'll need to accept and follow its guidance. You don't have to know everything. You just have to believe anything is possible and open yourself to receiving.

NINE OF SWORDS

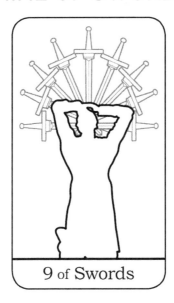

9 of Swords

The Nine of Swords tarot card is about anxiety, sleepless nights, and worry. Taken even further, it becomes about nightmares, isolation, and depression.

Traditionally, this card shows a woman sitting up in bed, with her hands covering her face. It's the middle of the night and she is clearly upset. Nine swords are hung on the wall behind her.

There is nothing good or hopeful here, unfortunately. Everyone feels the grief of the Nine of Swords at some time in their life, but most of us want to move past it as quickly as we can.

Sometimes we can get wrapped in a whirlpool of anxiety, regrets, and worry. The stress and guilt associated with rehashing past decisions and difficult situations can result in illness, mental suffering, and unhappiness.

Occasionally, this card indicates a hospital stay or rehab.

Keywords for the Nine of Swords Tarot Card
Depression, fear, anxiety
Nightmares, sleeplessness
Illness, hospital stays
Being too hard on yourself

Keywords for the Nine of Swords Reversed
Rest and recovery, healing
Time heals all wounds
Severe depression, torment

Patterns and Correspondences
The Swords = rules the mental and intellectual world
Suit of cards = spades
Timeline = hours to days
Number 9 = completion, wisdom attained
Zodiac sign = Gemini
Element = Air

Nine of Swords Reading for Love
None of the interpretations for this card are positive, unfortunately. In love, this card is about the hurtful words you wish you had left unsaid and the regret you feel afterward.

If you are having sleepless nights and anxiety because of your relationship, wake up and see the reality of your situation. Nothing will change until you make a decision and take action. Your first step is to look past your fears to see what actually is happening. It might not be as bad as you imagine!

And if it is, you have the strength and ability to change the situation. Quit stewing and start acting.

The Nine of Swords tarot card is a good indication that it's time to seek help. Find a therapist for yourself and approach your partner about couple counseling you can do together. It's an investment in making your relationship and your future stronger.

If you are looking for new love, stop being so hard on yourself for past mistakes. Leave your fears, anxiety, and worries behind you so you can start over.

You are exactly where you need to be right now. You are going to take the lessons from your past to help create a new healthy relationship. Start dreaming about how wonderful your future will be and leave your nightmares in the past.

Nine of Swords Reading for Work

Your work situation is not good and things do not look like they will get better without massive change.

Step outside of your situation and get advice from a neutral, uninvolved third party. Your fear, regrets, and anxiety are clouding your judgment.

No matter what happens, worrying about it won't make it change. Take care of yourself during these trying times and build something positive in at least one non-work-related area of your life (such as health, creative projects, or family relationships).

You can't control everything, but you can control your mental state. Get help if you need it.

Nine of Swords Reading for Health

It is time to seek help. Whenever you see the Nine of Swords, therapy is always a good idea.

Worrying ruins the present and doesn't help the future. The anxiety, unhappiness, and emotional pain of your (physical or mental) situation is making things worse.

Stress leads to sleeplessness and isolation, which leads to anxiety, illness, and depression. You are too far down the rabbit hole to claw your way out on your own. Stop making things so difficult for yourself. Ask for help.

There is no shame in this. It requires strength and courage to do what you fear. Admitting you need help is a courageous act.

Nine of Swords Reading for Money and Finances

You are swirling in a cesspool of worries, fear, and anxiety about money. To make matters worse, you are letting your past mistakes cloud your vision.

Things are different now, but you won't be able to see the options you have until you step out of the past and forgive yourself (and anyone else involved).

Your deepest fears of bankruptcy, being homeless, or losing your job are actually all survivable events. (They're awful events, for sure, but you will survive them).

You can't control or even predict what will happen in the future. But you can control your attitude today. You have a choice to stay stuck in your fears, worries, and stress or you can choose to think new, positive thoughts.

Ask for help. Admit the truth. Be brave and courageous and don't ever give up. You are much stronger than you think and change is just one thought away.

Nine of Swords Reading for Spiritual Guidance

This card indicates you are in too much mental pain to connect clearly with your spiritual side. You have to move past the fear, anxieties, and helplessness of your situation so you can ask for help.

Prayer, whatever form works for you, is a wonderful antidote to isolation and fear.

No matter how alone you feel, you aren't actually the only human being to have suffered in this way. And you always have the Universe (or God) on your side, even when you keep pushing help away.

Reaching out in prayer or meditation will give you perspective on your problems and will help you ask the right questions. These questions will lead you onto a new and brighter path.

TEN OF SWORDS

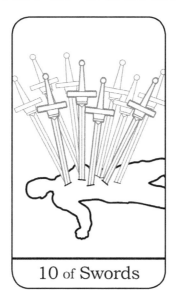

10 of Swords

The Ten of Swords, like many of the swords cards, has a generally negative and harsh message. This is the card for betrayal and hitting rock bottom, either due to your own actions or the actions of your enemies.

Just looking at this card, its meaning is clear. The Ten of Swords is about being stabbed in the back. Traditionally, this tarot card shows a dead man lying face-down on the ground, with ten bloody swords sticking out of his body.

Although the general meaning of this card is brutal, it also carries a message that the past is over. It no longer holds you and you are free to move in any new direction you choose. That's a freeing and positive thought!

You're in the muck right now, though. There is a sense of total loss and defeat and you are at the absolute bottom. This is a painful and unwanted ending, but you can't deny the situation any longer.

What is done is done. Your only option is to accept this fact and move on.

While there will be many tears and regret, once you put the past behind you and choose a future path, you will be able to move quickly onto something better.

Just because something is hard doesn't mean it is bad. This difficult and terrible situation will open the door for something new and wonderful to happen.

In a more literal sense, this card can indicate back pain, surgery, or relapsing back into addiction.

Keywords for the Ten of Swords Tarot Card
A complete and painful ending
Enemies, backstabbing, defeat
Hitting rock bottom, relapse
Back surgery or pain

Keywords for the Ten of Swords Reversed
Seeking redemption
Healing an old wound
Finding the courage to start over

Patterns and Correspondences
The Swords = rules the mental and intellectual world
Suit of cards = spades
Timeline = hours to days
Number 10 = beginning again with wisdom
Zodiac sign = Gemini
Element = Air

Ten of Swords Reading for Love
No good news here, unfortunately. The Ten of Swords tarot card indicates a complete and painful ending, with the added bonus of betrayal and crisis. This does not bode well if you are struggling to maintain a relationship. This card isn't a guarantee for a breakup, but you are facing the ending of something. It may be the end of the relationship, but it may be the end of a phase or role in your life.

This is a difficult time, but whatever happens will open the door to something better. Wallowing in the heartbreak will draw out your pain. Accept what has happened and let it go. Forgiveness is required, not optional.

If you are looking for new love, it is imperative you release and forgive all of your past partners and love role-models. You will be unable to move into a healthy relationship unless you completely move on from your past.

You would benefit from therapy or counseling to identify the beliefs and patterns keeping you stuck.

Overall, expect communication to be blocked and difficult.

TEN OF SWORDS READING FOR WORK

You have enemies at work who are working behind the scenes to damage your reputation. Unfortunately, if they are successful, there isn't much you can do other than accept the defeat, learn your lessons, and move on.

The best revenge will be to start over with gratitude, joy, and a bigger, better plan. You don't ever have to stoop to their level. They will stay stuck mired in their manipulations and gossip, and you will rise above their petty fears to create a life they can only dream about.

Keep your standards high and keep your focus on the future. Let the past go.

You must forgive yourself for all of your past mistakes and personal failings. They are in the past and you are now a new person. You have learned from your mistakes and grown stronger.

Open yourself up to completely new opportunities and don't taint the present by holding on to grudges or expectations from the past.

Ten of Swords Reading for Health

This card often indicates back pain or surgery. If you are suffering from pain or problems, the only remedy is to seek help. You can't fix these problems on your own. Consider alternative options like acupuncture, massage, or yoga before jumping straight into surgery. Do everything you can to get this problem solved.

If you are carrying old resentments, grudges, and bitter feelings toward people or events in your past, please release them. The stress and negativity is affecting your health (even if it doesn't seem like it). You must release the past so you can move on to a better future.

Ten of Swords Reading for Money and Finances

Keep your money close and don't trust anyone who offers you an investment that seems too good to be true. Even your closest friends and family can betray you (intentionally or by mistake).

If you have made horrendous financial decisions in the past, forgive yourself and begin to take small steps in the present to improve your situation. Forgiveness is an on-going habit, so continue to release your past pains as you build your new future.

Starting over is actually a blessing. This time, you'll have the benefit of the lessons you've learned, the mistakes you've made, and the knowledge you've gained. You are ready to create wealth and true financial security.

Ten of Swords Reading for Spiritual Guidance

Before you can attend to spiritual matters, you must forgive yourself and the others who have hurt you. You can't live in the past and at the same time expect to be present in your life. It's one or the other. Meditation and prayer will help, but the key is forgiveness.

You only have one moment - this moment - to live your life. Don't waste this precious time by holding on tightly to something that no longer exists. Once the past no longer holds you, you are free to move in a new direction toward what matters. You'll be able to live your life with joy and purpose, without the pain, weight, and stress you're currently carrying.

PAGE OF SWORDS

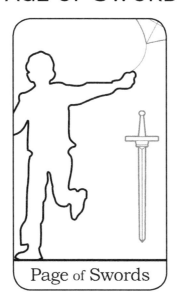

Page of Swords

The Page of Swords is the naughtiest of the Page cards. This card often represents someone seen as a "problem child." They aren't a bad person, just someone who is talkative, curious, strong-willed, and spirited. He or she will push up against boundaries and rules, and may live outside of society's accepted standards.

The Page of Swords, like all the court cards, can be interpreted as an actual person, as a role you play, or as a message. If it is an actual person in your life, it will be a stubborn, curious, talkative person with youthful energy.

In the traditional RW-based deck, the Page of Swords card shows a young man holding sword in the air. The sword is almost as big as he is! All of the Swords court cards have birds flying in the background, symbolizing the Air element for this card.

The Air element represents logic, the intellect, and verbal communication. This card often carries a message about mounting a legal defense, making an oath, or revealing deception and secrets. No matter what, the sword will cut through the lies and the truth will soon be revealed.

The Page of Swords is a practical thinker. When you are ready to create a step-by-step action plan to get the job done, this is someone you want in your life.

Occasionally, this card can mean someone is keeping the truth hidden from you or has a hidden agenda. This card is also associated with spies, gossips, and prying eyes.

Keywords for the Page of Swords Tarot Card
A talkative and strong-willed youthful person
Gossip, spying, or prying eyes
Delayed or upsetting news
Mounting a legal defense

Keywords for the Page of Swords Reversed
All talk and no action
A bratty or immature child
Legal or tax issues

Patterns and Correspondences
The Swords = rules the mental and intellectual world
Suit of cards = spades
Timeline = hours to days
The Page = info and messages to grow new understanding
Element = Air

Page of Swords Reading for Love
If you are looking for love, keep your eyes out for someone who is talkative and curious about you and your life. They may be younger than you or have youthful energy.

If you are in a relationship, something may be hidden from you. Be patient. The truth will soon come out. Until then, forget your doubts and do the work. The Page of Swords likes action, not just information, so be the relationship partner you would like to have.

To take on the role of the Page of Swords in your love life and become curious about the world around you. Search out new hobbies, activities, and people. Do things outside of your comfort zone. Treat dating and your relationship like a fun game, without pressure, manipulation, or expectation of any kind.

PAGE OF SWORDS READING FOR WORK

The Page of Swords is constantly learning, but this isn't only book-knowledge. This Page is eager to put information into action. Sometimes that eager energy means the Page acts without a plan or road map. This reckless action will not bring positive results.

Someone in your life (maybe even you) needs to be warned to be cautious. The Page of Swords excels at creating detailed action plans. Rein in your eagerness and excitement to create a plan that will bring results.

Although some action is required, be sure you know the complete picture before you make a decision. Something may be hidden or delayed, so create a complete step-by-step road map while you wait for more information.

PAGE OF SWORDS READING FOR HEALTH

This is a card of decisive action paired with practical thinking. If you are struggling with your health, you can't wish yourself to be better. You must create a plan and then take step-by-step daily action to improve your situation.

If there is a Page of Swords in your life, ask them for guidance or to be your accountability buddy. They have more than enough energy for the both of you!

As this card can sometimes indicate unseen problems coming to light, get a complete physical and full panel of blood work. Don't be afraid of the results. Once you know your true situation, you can become the Page of Swords and create a plan of attack.

PAGE OF SWORDS READING FOR MONEY

Do not make any investments at this time. There is delayed, upsetting, or hidden information. Until you have the truth and understand everyone's involvement, do not make any decisions.

Money loves direction, however, so this is a wonderful time to create an action plan for how you will improve your financial situation and build wealth.

Take small actions on a daily basis, going step-by-step to bring you closer to your goals. Create and follow a simple budget or spending plan and brainstorm small but actionable ways you can increase your income.

Page of Swords Reading for Spiritual Guidance

If there is someone in your life who is talkative, strong-willed, stubborn, and curious, they may be able to guide you deeper into your spiritual path.

This Page of Swords may be a challenging person in your life, but that's a good thing. We gain strength when things are difficult, not when things are easy. This Page will help you practice the spiritual lessons of unconditional love, forgiveness, compassion, and service.

You can also model yourself on the Page of Swords by constantly learning and putting your lessons into daily action. Forget your doubts (about yourself, your guides, or your path) and do the work on a daily basis.

This could mean regular meditation, talking with spiritual advisers, or reading the books of your faith. Set a plan and a schedule for how you will integrate these spiritual activities into your routine and your life.

Knight of Swords

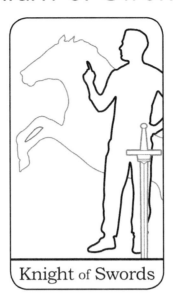

Knight of Swords

The Knight of Swords tarot card shows a knight riding a horse into battle without hesitation. His sword is held in front of him as he charges forward decisively.

Like all court cards, this one can represent an actual person in your life, a role you are ready to play, or a message. In all interpretations, it is an extremely active card.

The Knight of Swords can represent a soldier, a fearless crusader, or any youthful person who enters your life quickly to stir it up. Whoever this Knight is, it is someone who charges forward and acts quickly. They hate to be held back.

This Knight is forceful, assertive, and works hard to be heard and understood. He or she is always on the move and is often seen as being rash and impulsive.

He's generally not actually rash or impulsive, however. He just thinks faster than the rest of us! He is a master of passionate thinking and creatively considers every option quickly before deciding on a course of action.

If you pull the Knight of Swords, you may have to make a quick decision and take immediate action to make it happen. Create your own path. Don't spend the time searching for the easiest or most common way. Make your own way.

Occasionally, this card can represent travel by air or a change in lifestyle.

KEYWORDS FOR THE KNIGHT OF SWORDS TAROT CARD
A soldier or fearless crusader
Quick action toward a goal
Bold communication
Travel by air

KEYWORDS FOR THE KNIGHT OF SWORDS REVERSED
Violence, abuse, deliberate cruelty
Someone out of control
Passive-aggressive behavior

PATTERNS AND CORRESPONDENCES
The Swords = rules the mental and intellectual world
Suit of cards = spades
Timeline = hours to days
The Knight = learning and testing new wisdom
Element = Air

KNIGHT OF SWORDS READING FOR LOVE
If you are looking for love, be forewarned that the Knight of Swords will boldly enter your life just to stir it up. Keep your eyes out for a fast-talking, fast-thinking person. If this new person desires a relationship, they will quickly take action to make it happen. You can let yourself be swept off your feet, but also trust your instincts and your intuition.

For advice about an existing relationship, take lessons from this Knight. Cut to the chase and speak your mind. Do not hem and haw or dance around the issues. Be the one to take bold action. Clearly communicate your needs and desires.

Knight of Swords Reading for Work

If there is no obvious person in your work life who has the qualities of the Knight of Swords, you may be ready to take on this Knight's qualities yourself. Become assertive and stay alert for projects where you can act quickly and cut your own path.

Someone (possibly you) is working very hard to be heard. Be sure you are listening as well as clearly communicating your bold plans and ideas.

If you have a creative or unusual idea for a business, project, or opportunity, pursue it quickly. Follow the quick-acting advice of this Knight and build your business backward. Before creating the product or service, find customers who are willing to buy it.

See who wants your solution and what they will pay. Once you have guaranteed buyers, get them to invest in your idea. Move quickly and don't get bogged down with creating the "perfect solution."

Knight of Swords Reading for Health

This is a card of action. If you are struggling with your health, you must change your lifestyle. Nothing about this situation will change until you change your beliefs, thoughts, choices, actions, and behaviors.

Change your habits and act differently than you have in the past. Find creative solutions and put them into action.

This is an extremely active card, so consider outdoor activities, gym classes, and sports to get you moving. Walking is fantastic, but so is hiking up a mountain to see the sunrise!

Take charge of your life and you will be able to change it. The only excuses standing in your way are the ones you allow into your life. Ignore the excuses (or work around them) and you will see radical, positive change.

Knight of Swords Reading for Money

Money loves clarity and action. Create your own financial plan and put the plan into action quickly. Stay alert for opportunities and do the daily work to mind your money responsibly.

Do not jump into any rash financial decisions and beware the fast-talking get-rich-quick guys who act like the Knight of Swords (but really are just charlatans in disguise).

Use the Knight's sword to cut through your lifestyle expenses. Take bold action to remove everything that doesn't bring you joy and serve your values. Spend your money only on the things that deeply matter to you, even if it means you are living a lifestyle that seems strange to your friends and neighbors.

Financially, things will start happening faster than you expect. Make sure your movement is in a positive direction and not toward debt, bad investments, or poor choices. Your daily habits matter. Every single action counts.

Knight of Swords Reading for Spirituality

The Knight of Swords is about action, not reflection. However, an active spiritual life involves more than meditation and prayer.

It's important you live your beliefs. This means integrating your spiritual practices into your daily life, making choices aligned with your values, and treating everyone (including yourself) with unconditional respect and compassion.

Use the Knight of Swords as a role model to become a fearless crusader of the truth. Your spiritual path is unique to you and will not align with traditional or conventional religion. The way you live your life will be an inspiration to others who are searching for their own spiritual alignment.

Queen of Swords

Queen of Swords

The Queen of Swords tarot card, like all court cards, often represents an actual person in your life. It can also mean a role you are playing or need to play. If this is an actual person, it will be a man or woman who is a fierce protector.

Traditionally, this card shows a strong and beautiful woman sitting on a throne. She is holding a sword upright in her right hand and she is gesturing with her left hand. The throne, the crown, and her dress are covered with butterflies.

The Queen of Swords is a perceptive and independent person. She might be a widow, widower, or has otherwise suffered loss, loneliness, and grief. These lessons have taught her to be shrewd, stern, and impartial in her love.

This Queen is logical, intellectual, and never acts rashly. You may not like her - in fact, many people think she's a cold bitch - but she is always objective and fair. Her heart is in the right place.

This woman calls things as they are and is fearless critic of ignorance, unfairness, and injustice. While she is often frightening, it is safe to take your mask off around her. She loves the underdog and accept reality, including the weaknesses and failures of herself and others. Do not fear making a mistake in front of her. Just don't ever make the same mistake twice!

Keywords for the Queen of Swords Tarot Card
A self-sufficient, logical person
Someone deeply concerned with fairness
Someone who has suffered loss, loneliness, or grief
Speaking the truth

Keywords for the Queen of Swords Reversed
Someone who is bitter and negative
Cold, heartless logic
Acting without compassion

Patterns and Correspondences
The Swords = rules the mental and intellectual world
Suit of cards = spades
Timeline = hours to days
The Queen = inner wisdom and mastery
Element = Air

Queen of Swords Reading for Love
The Queen of Swords is extremely independent, so this is not always a good card for love. You may be ready to learn a few lessons from her about standing on your own, trusting your judgment, and entertaining yourself in solitude.

However, you might also find yourself falling for a someone who is logical, intellectual, and loyal. This person doesn't like to be controlled or directed, but if you give them freedom to make up their own mind, they will be incredibly loving and loyal toward you and the people who are important to you.

If you are in a relationship, take advice from this Queen to tell the truth, even when it hurts. Her sword can cut through anything.

Be compassionate, honest, and brave. You will learn exactly what you need to know and you will have the strength to act on it.

Queen of Swords Reading for Work

The Queen of Swords makes a wonderful mentor. She (or he) will help you see through the politics and bullshit at work and will show you the path toward service and success.

If you have someone like this in your professional life, you are very lucky. They may be difficult to work with or for - in fact, you might not like them. But you will respect them and that is more important.

This mentor will not compromise their values. Ever. They will always willingly live with the consequences of their actions, knowing they are just, fair, and true. This doesn't make them popular, but it does make them a trusted member of the team.

If you are faced with a problem at work, you already know the answer. Call things as they are and take action to correct anything unfair or unjust. Think clearly and then act decisively.

Queen of Swords Reading for Health

The Queen of Swords wants you to become more self-sufficient. You have been relying on the ideas and efforts of others for too long.

While you do need a support system and professional help, they can't do the work for you. You must take action, daily, even when you don't want to.

This Queen is a strong, fierce, independent crusader. When you struggle, imagine you are the Queen of Swords and let her passion and commitment drive you to action. Never back down on your goal, no matter what happens. It doesn't matter if it takes four months or four years, as long as you never give up.

Queen of Swords Reading for Money

This Queen does not make rash or impulsive decisions. She logically and impartially looks through all sides of a choice before making a decision. Once she makes her decision, however, she acts quickly and without regret.

She is also deeply concerned with fairness, so everyone involved (including yourself!) must be treated fairly with any financial decision you make. Your financial security is as valuable as anyone else's. How do you think she got to be so independent in the first place?

A good place to start is with your own salary. Men commonly earn about 30% more than women, partly because they ask for more money. Set a date to ask for a raise and begin practicing your negotiation skills. If you are self-employed, set a date to raise your prices and begin preparing your clients and audience for the increase.

Queen of Swords Reading for Spirituality

The Queen of Swords is as perceptive as she is independent. She follows the beating of her own heart, instead of blindly following the crowd. She is also extremely concerned with treating everyone justly and fairly.

Take a good, hard look at your own life, especially the conversations you have and the daily actions you take (or don't take). If you are not living your life and creating habits in line with your spiritual values, you are letting yourself and the world down.

The details matter. How you praise your children, thank the mail carrier, celebrate small successes, discipline the dog, congratulate a co-worker, care for your skin, sign off on your emails, and fold the laundry all contribute to who you are and what you add to the world. Your small choices must align with your values and spiritual understanding. Live each moment in alignment.

KING OF SWORDS

King of Swords

The King of Swords, like all of the court cards, can indicate an actual person, a role you play, or a message. The King of Swords tarot card represents a thoughtful leader who is a master of intentional behavior and analytical thought.

Traditionally, this card shows a man sitting proudly on a throne, holding a sword in his right hand. He's wearing a crown and a fancy robe.

If this card is representing an actual person in your life, look for a person (male or female) who is forceful, decisive, and blunt. They will be a powerful leader in their professional life and might wear a uniform.

The King of Swords is as good with words as he is with thought and action. This is the type of person who will carefully think through a decision and be intentional in their actions. They clearly visualize what they want, need, and desire, and then take immediate and decisive action to get it.

If this card represents a role you play in your life, you must get your head, heart, and actions in alignment. You have the power to make great choices, but don't rush.

Do your homework, examine your choices from all sides, and then take decisive action to see them through.

Keywords for the King of Swords Tarot Card
An analytical person who communicates well
Someone in uniform
Ruled by the head, not the emotions
Fairness and truth

Keywords for the King of Swords Reversed
Mental exhaustion
Logic that turns to cruelty
Corrupt politician, con man, or a cynic

Patterns and Correspondences
The Swords = rules the mental and intellectual world
Suit of cards = spades
Timeline = hours to days
The King = expanding and sharing wisdom
Element = Air

King of Swords Reading for Love
The King of Swords tarot card is about clarity of thought and clear, honest communication. While this card doesn't indicate a lusty and passionate romance, it points to a relationship that will last if both parties are committed to compromise, honesty, and compassion.

If you desire a new relationship, be on the lookout for someone in uniform or a decisive leader to cross your path. This will be a person who is ruled more by their head than their heart (at least outwardly), so be prepared to eloquently state your case why the two of you should be together.

You may need to be the instigator of the relationship. If you don't feel comfortable making the first move, be clear on your attraction and interest. Flirting is fun, but it is better to build trust and respect between the two of you.

The King of Swords is attracted to a partner who can understand their need for fair, logical, and direct communication. This is someone who will appreciate your honesty and be compassionate toward your vulnerability.

If you are in a relationship, use the King of Swords as a role model for your own behavior. The King visualizes exactly what he wants to happen in any situation before taking action. Do the same when dealing with any difficult situation or conversation you need to have. You can't let problems sit and stew. You must immediately address them and create a plan together to move on.

KING OF SWORDS READING FOR WORK

The King of Swords may represent your boss at work or some other professional authority figure. If you have a King in your life, go to them for career advice. Present a carefully designed plan and ask for feedback. Be prepared with clear questions. And when they give you advice, be sure to take it! Follow up with them later with your results. You'll win a fan for life.

If you don't have a King of Swords in your professional life, take on the qualities of this King. Be analytical and thoughtful in your decisions and take quick and decisive action once your choice is made. Be completely fair and just in all you do. Always take the high road and never compromise your honesty, integrity, or values.

KING OF SWORDS READING FOR HEALTH

This king is extremely intentional about how he (or she) approaches all aspects of life. This is the type of person who wakes at 5am every morning for a swim before work and rigidly drinks only one glass of wine at dinner, never more.

The King of Swords spends time thinking through every decision, carefully considering all the alternatives and consequences. Once he makes a decision, he sticks with it. Can you say the same?

Take an honest review of your daily habits and routines. If you are avoiding daily exercise, eating junk food, living off caffeine and sugar and adrenaline, or otherwise treating yourself poorly, you have to make changes. The changes will be easier than you think, but you have to get started today.

King of Swords Reading for Money and Finances

If you are struggling with your finances, turn to someone in your life who can act as a mentor. The King of Swords is extremely good with money and financial decisions. He (or she) will help you think through and take action on your decisions.

You have complete control over your life, even if it doesn't feel that way. The King of Swords can guide you to analyze the pros and cons of your choices and point you toward the logical and rational next step. With this King's help, you have the power to change your own life.

King of Swords Reading for Spiritual Guidance

This card is not usually seen as a spiritual card, however the King of Swords is often very spiritual and will credit his success to outside forces. This is both humility and truth.

The King of Swords listens to his intuition, but always runs his ideas through his rational mind as well. Using intuition, your gut, or your inner wisdom is vitally important, but not at the expense of logic or analytical thought. You need both to be whole.

Don't neglect your intellectual mind. Learn new ideas from ancient philosophy, classic novels, and deep conversations with people who intimidate you. Your spiritual life will grow when you allow these unconventional outside ideas into your life.

ACE OF WANDS

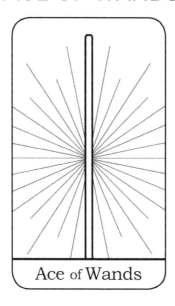

Ace of Wands

The Ace of Wands tarot card is definitely a good omen. It is the "hell yeah - go for it!" card. It pops up at the beginning of a new hot and sexy relationship or at the beginning of an awesome new job or creative project. When you need a new and innovative solution to a problem or want to pull ideas "out of thin air," this is the card you want to see.

The Ace of Wands is the spark of something new, combining the wood of the wand with the element of fire to blaze something big into being.

It blazes with the urge to create. It could be a new career, a new baby, a new relationship, or a new direction in your life.

This card thrusts quickly with a desire to bring something new into being. It's a lusty and action-oriented card. If you're starting a new relationship, keep the wand under wraps if you don't want a child!

KEYWORDS FOR THE ACE OF WANDS TAROT CARD
New life, vitality, conception
The urge to create
A new career, project, or idea
The start of something amazing

Keywords for the Ace of Wands Reversed
A false start, delays
Things are not ready
Impotence issues

Patterns and Correspondences
The Wands = rules the personality, ego, and personal power
Suit of cards = clubs
Timeline = days to weeks
Number 1 = new beginnings, starting on a journey
Element = Fire

Ace of Wands Reading for Love
This is an excellent card for love. If you are looking for a new relationship, something sexy and incredible is just around the corner. Follow your passions, interests, and desires and don't let fear hold you back. This one is going to burn HOT!

This is an action-oriented card, though, so you must put yourself out there. Be an active participant in the process by setting up an online dating profile, saying "yes" to every invitation, and making the effort to try new things. Attend local MeetUps, sign up for a class or new activity, and schedule your social calendar with fun, new events. When you chase your passions, passion will chase you.

If you are in an existing relationship, this card is a cue to bring new life into your partnership. No more boring dinner-and-a-movie dates, or lazing in front of the computer or TV all weekend! Spice things up (in and out of the bedroom) by getting creative and finding fun and ridiculously silly new things to try together.

If you want to start or grow your family, this card is 100% supportive. Go for it!

Ace of Wands Reading for Work
Your dream job or project is headed your way. The Ace of Wands card carries the spark of a new endeavor, but you will have to follow it and bring it to life.

If there has been a passion project you've been putting on the back burner, this is the time to pursue it. Fit it around the edges of your daily routine if you must, and keep the project quiet if you don't think you'll have support. But once the project gets going, it will catch fire on its own and blaze into success.

Take the initiative and get creative about how you approach your daily habits and routine. You will need confidence and courage to follow your passion, but it will absolutely be worth it. Put yourself out there into new and challenging situations. You will thrive in a position or responsibility that is "over your head." You are much more capable than you think.

ACE OF WANDS READING FOR HEALTH

The Ace of Wands is a good omen for health, especially if you've been stuck in rut or have plateaued in your fitness or weight-loss goals.

The key is to let go of what has worked in the past or what works for other people. You are a unique and special snowflake and you must find the path, habits, and support system that works for you.

Look for innovative approaches or solutions to your health problems and shake up your routine by following your passions instead of following the crowd. This means trying new things until you find the fitness activities, cooking and eating routines, and lifestyle changes that light you up and fill you with joy and energy.

ACE OF WANDS READING FOR MONEY AND FINANCES

If you are looking to invest your money in a new project, this card is a good sign. Be careful, of course, but the return will be high if you focus on bringing your passions to life.

This isn't "win the lottery" money or passive income. You'll have to do a lot of work to make this investment happen. But if it's work you love, it's the right path for you.

If you are struggling financially, just stop. Stop repeating the mistakes and habits of the past. Stop spending money you don't have. Stop pretending things will get better on their own. These things are obviously not working! You will want to create new habits and systems to help you save and spend wisely.

Your money is your vote on what you want to exist in the world. Your spending (and your income and your investments) must align with your values.

ACE OF WANDS READING FOR SPIRITUAL GUIDANCE

Your intuition is on fire! Ideas are coming fast and furiously and you are easily able to bring them into action in your daily life.

This card is the spark for something new and includes new directions and thoughts on your spiritual path. The Ace of Wands is your cue to start following your own path, not the traditional or common route.

Follow your heart and dive right into your deepest, scariest desires and hidden thoughts. When you integrate them together, they'll bring you to wholeness. By bringing awareness to what you love, desire, and fear, you will discover a deeper compassion and unconditional love for yourself. This will be the start of a radical, life-long, amazing love affair with yourself that will change your life.

TWO OF WANDS

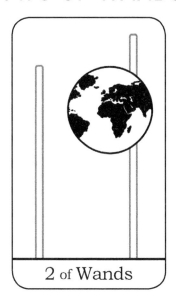

The Two of Wands tarot is a positive card about the uncomfortable-yet-exciting period of creative tension and hopeful waiting that happens before any big project.

In the RW-based tarot deck, the Two of Wands shows a man holding a globe in one hand as he stares into the distance. He is gripping one wand and the other is attached to the wall behind him. The Two of Wands indicates favorable prospects, but only if you take control of the situation.

This card is about waiting, planning, and wise decision making. It's a positive card about setting strong intentions and expectations.

You have more than one option, so start doing research, making plans, and creating the road map to lead you into the future.

Decisive action will be needed to realize your goals, so prepare yourself. You are ready to make a decision and choose a future path. No more waffling or waiting or hoping things will get better. If you want things to change - YOU must change. Start by making a solid plan.

This card can also indicate travel, planning your next trip, or a desire to see the world.

Many people confuse the meaning of this card with the Three of Wands, since the images and meanings are similar. This card is about the planning and decisions before you take action and the Three of Wands is more about the waiting period after action has been taken.

Keywords for the Two of Wands Tarot Card
Future planning
A period of waiting
Creative tension
The need to choose a path
Travel or the desire to see the world

Keywords for the Two of Wands Reversed
Doubt
Fear of the unknown
Delay or cancellation of a trip or project
Finish what you've started

Patterns and Correspondences
The Wands = rules the personality, ego, and personal power
Suit of cards = clubs
Timeline = days to weeks
Number 2 = balance and pairings
Zodiac sign = Aries
Element = Fire

Two of Wands Reading for Love
If you are looking for a new relationship, you can't sit around waiting for a new partner to be delivered to your door. You must create a plan to meet new people and let yourself be seen.

How will you expand your social life? What type of relationship are you looking for? What qualities do you want in a partner? How can you live those qualities in your own life?

You can't go after what you want until you determine what that is. Once you know the answers, create a plan to put yourself into the environments where you can find what you desire.

For existing relationships, start making future plans with your partner. This card indicates a favorable outcome, so don't be afraid to ask the big questions!

Two of Wands Reading for Work

Career-wise, you have more than one option and you can no longer rest on your laurels or the successes of the past. Create your own future instead of letting things push you along. You've skated so far, but things will become a struggle if you continue on this same path. You must take action and do something different.

Identify the multiple paths you could take, then choose the best one. Be prepared to take decisive action and firmly close the doors of the past behind you. Remove and eliminate what isn't working so you'll have the space and time available to take action when the time comes.

The Two of Wands can also indicate expanding your business or career internationally, or taking a business trip. If you've been thinking of going global, now is the time!

Two of Wands Reading for Health

If you are struggling with your health, you can't wait any longer. Create a plan and make the choice to take care of your body. No one will do it for you.

Consult with a professional and have them put a plan together with you. Trust their guidance, but make sure the plan meets your needs and personal goals.

Soon, you will have to commit to seeing things through. But for now, begin with baby steps. Ask for help, brainstorm options, and put together a realistic plan.

The change will start slowly, but it will be for the better. To see success, set strong intentions and then follow through.

Two of Wands Reading for Money and Finances

The Two of Wands is about planning for the future, with an emphasis on security and success. Don't make any huge investments or purchases until you understand how they will impact your long-term financial situation.

If you are struggling financially, it's time to take control. What worked in the past no longer works for you, so start making new plans and investigating new options. Create a road map toward financial security and then follow it.

This card is about creating a solid, actionable, and do-able plan you will actually implement. Prepare yourself (physically and emotionally) to begin implementing that plan of good financial habits.

Money loves a good plan and it loves action even more! Be the one to take charge of your money and tell it where to go. Yes, this means creating a budget at the start of each month. Take a look at YNAB - You Need A Budget if you need help getting your finances in order.

Two of Wands Reading for Spiritual Guidance

The Two of Wands tarot card indicates progress, decisions, and discovery.

You are ready to identify and follow your own path, even if it leads you off the conventional route. You have many options and all are quite good, but you must find the one meant for you.

Make a decision so you can move forward. Staying stuck in indecision and possibilities won't get you closer to your goals. Even if you choose the wrong path, you will learn and experience more than if you stay stuck.

THREE OF WANDS

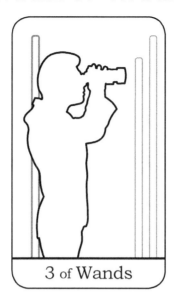

3 of Wands

The Three of Wands tarot card arrives when you've made all the right moves and are waiting for the results. You'll soon be rewarded for your efforts, but this is a period of waiting.

It's also a card about collaboration and teamwork, especially in business.

In the RW-based tarot deck, this card shows a man gazing off into the distance at three ships sailing at sea. Three wands are stuck in the ground behind him.

He's watching his ships come in. His partner is on one of the boats filled with wonderful cargo and he's watching them pull into the harbor to find out how much money they've made.

When you are awaiting the results of your prior actions, you can feel confident success is coming to you. It's likely this success will bring the possibility for a major expansion of your plans and visions. Dream big!

Occasionally, this card also indicates travel.

Keywords for the Three of Wands Tarot Card

Commerce, expansion
Success is coming!
Preparation and foresight
Collaboration, teamwork

Keywords for the Three of Wands Reversed

Delays and obstacles
Current plans not working out
Go back to the original vision

Patterns and Correspondences

The Wands = rules the personality, ego, and personal power
Suit of cards = clubs
Timeline = days to weeks
Number 3 = creating reality
Zodiac sign = Aries
Element = Fire

Three of Wands Reading for Love

The Three of Wands is about business and commerce, not love. However, this card does indicate a collaboration or partnership of two people working toward a common goal, so you can read it positively during a love reading.

You must do the work, though! You can't sit around waiting for good things to happen. The Three of Wands is about waiting for results after you've put in the hard work. Get down to business to build the partnership you want to have.

If you are looking for a new relationship, you must model the behavior and lifestyle of the partnership you want to have. Don't go looking for a one-night-stand at the Bible Study book group and don't go looking for a new wife at the Bridal Dress Shop. Put yourself into the environments where you are likely to find the type of relationship and type of person you desire.

If you are in an existing relationship, focus on working toward shared goals together. Find a big project you can work on and turn the project into a fun activity. Build memories as you strengthen your relationship.

Three of Wands Reading for Work

This is an extremely positive card for work, especially involving a partnership or group project.

If you are looking for a new opportunity, you must do the work to make things happen. Maintain constant focus and stay the course until the project comes to completion.

Any new venture or major expansion involving other people is a good idea. Do the work, think big, pull your weight, and stay positive. Be patient, but your actions will show great results.

Three of Wands Reading for Health

If you are waiting to hear news or see improvements in your health, keep taking positive action as you wait. The news will be positive, so don't give up now!

Continue moving toward your goals and maintain good habits. If you have the opportunity, partner with someone who has similar goals. This could mean finding the right doctor or fitness trainer, or by partnering with a friend to go to the gym each morning. Teamwork and collaboration is the right choice.

Three of Wands Reading for Money

If you have been taking positive action with your finances, you will soon see great results. The preparation, foresight, and planning you've already put forth will bring the rewards to you.

If you are struggling with your finances, partner with someone who knows more than you. Find a financial adviser or mentor who has the success you want. They will have advice and clues for you to follow, but it is your responsibility to follow their advice. You must make the right moves before you see results.

Changing your financial future will not happen overnight, but if you take small, regular steps in the right direction, it will change for the better. Keep doing the work and never give up.

Three of Wands Reading for Spiritual Guidance

This card is more practical and mundane than spiritual, but you can use its traditional meanings of partnership, collaboration, and teamwork to interpret it.

Find someone who can be a spiritual partner to help you along your path. This might mean directly connecting with a religious figure or reaching out to a study group who can mentor you as you go deeper into your own spiritual journey.

Consider turning to books, podcasts, and online communities if your local community doesn't support your path. You may want to look broader for the inspiration you need.

FOUR OF WANDS

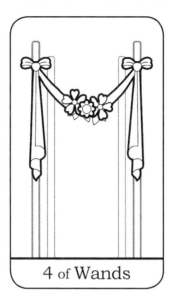

4 of Wands

The Four of Wands tarot card is a celebration of love, friendship, and family. Traditionally, this card shows two women dancing with flowers in their hands. In the foreground, four large wands are connected by a flower garland, creating an archway or trellis for their party.

It is an extremely positive card if you are looking to settle down and create a safe haven and happy home for yourself and others.

The Four of Wands is a fantastic card for love and can indicate a wedding or moving in together with your partner. This is also the card for reunions, homecomings, celebrations, and parties with friends.

Things in your life are all starting to come together and you have built a strong foundation. There is the potential for something even better, but for now celebrate all you have.

Occasionally, this card indicates relocation or moving to a new home, or some other life transition.

Keywords for the Four of Wands Tarot Card
A safe haven and happy home
Wedding, marriage, community
Celebration, party, or homecoming
Friendship
Relocation or moving

Keywords for the Four of Wands Reversed
Transitions, change
Breakdown in communication
Moving out or leaving home
A surprise party

Patterns and Correspondences
The Wands = rules the personality, ego, and personal power
Suit of cards = clubs
Timeline = days to weeks
Number 4 = practical foundations
Zodiac sign = Aries
Element = Fire

Four of Wands Reading for Love
This is a great card for love! If you are looking for a new relationship, attend any and every social event your friends and family invite you to. Let everyone know you are available and willing to be set-up. Your next partner is likely connected to your existing social circle in some way.

If you are looking to deepen an existing relationship, all signs point toward creating a happy home together. Weddings, marriage, and family are all connected to this card.

If you want to deepen your relationship, start by having conversations focused on long-term goals and plans. You'll want to know you are on the same page and the same timeline before you invest more effort into this relationship. All signs point toward a fun celebration, so this will likely be a very positive conversation.

Four of Wands Reading for Work

When it comes to your work and career, the Four of Wands is a positive omen. You have been experiencing small victories and building your foundation for success. It looks like something even better is on its way!

Things are starting to come together for you and there is the potential for something even bigger. Celebrate your successes with the people who have helped you and make sure they feel appreciated and recognized.

This card can indicate a life transition or change, so if you are looking to change careers or jobs, it will be a positive move.

Four of Wands Reading for Health

Get in the daily flow of making small, positive changes to your life and celebrate every victory, no matter how small. Keep doing the work to build your health. Every little bit makes a difference and this card says your work is paying off.

When it comes to your health, you can't make any significant, long-lasting change without involving others. You will need their advice, ideas, and support as you take daily action toward your goals.

If you are feeling unstable in regards to your health, turn to your friends and family. Create a safe haven with the people who love you. Involve your friends and ask them (in very specific ways) to support you. Consider hiring a personal trainer or coach to help you set goals and celebrate your successes.

Four of Wands Reading for Money and Finances

The Four of Wands wants you to celebrate where you are, right now. You don't need a lot of money to throw a great party! Have a potluck and invite the people who are key to your support network. Tell them your plans and ask for their support. They want to see you succeed, so share your appreciation and enthusiasm with the people who love you most.

Each positive choice you repeatedly make (to make more money, to use a budget, to pay off debt, to spend less than you earn, and to invest wisely) is a brick building the foundation of your financial future.

Celebrate every financial victory, even if it's something as small as opening a savings account for the first time. Celebrations are best shared and don't have to be expensive. Get creative with how you reward your good actions. Ask your friends or family if they have ideas for how you can build wealth together.

Four of Wands Reading for Spiritual Guidance

The Four of Wands is a practical card about the real-world matters of family, friendship, and community.

This may seem at odds with a spiritual message, but searching for your spiritual path is really a search for connection. Don't discount the lessons your friends and family have to teach you, especially if your faith and spiritual beliefs are different. In fact, it's the differences that will help you practice putting your spiritual beliefs into action.

It's easy to be open-minded and nonjudgmental when everyone looks, believes, and acts like you do. But that isn't what you need.

Put yourself into new environments to expose yourself to fresh ideas, different cultures, and other faiths. When your own beliefs are challenged, you will strengthen your beliefs and practice your values at the same time.

If you have found a spiritual or religious community that feels safe, celebrate! Become an energetic member of your community by welcoming new members, honoring the shared traditions, and participating in the events that make your faith special. Be an active and enthusiastic member of the communities that inspire you.

FIVE OF WANDS

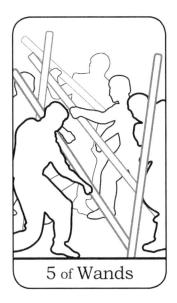

5 of Wands

The Five of Wands tarot card is about the positive challenges you face when you are in conflict or competition with others.

While conflict, rivalry, and strife seem like negative things, they are opportunities for growth. You're going to have to suit up and fight. There's no hiding any more.

When you see this card in a tarot spread, you are ready to go All In and commit with total focus and discipline. Win or lose, you'll at least know you gave it your all, which is the ultimate success. GO ALL IN.

Most of us do "just enough" to get the job done, without ever committing to see what our full potential actually looks like. With the Five of Wands, you must commit beyond anything you've done before. This is radical change, discipline, and focus. And with your radical commitment, you'll see radical growth.

In the traditional RW-based tarot deck, the Five of Wands shows five young men fighting, each with a wand in their hands. From the expressions on their faces, this feels more like play-fighting than real violence.

This card is about competition, rivalry, and sport. It's a positive, fun, and active card. In some cases, this card can represent interpersonal bonding, sports, or even sexual play.

Keywords for the Five of Wands Tarot Card
Interpersonal bonding, sport, rivalry
Competition
Conflict, challenge
Confrontation

Keywords for the Five of Wands Reversed
Harmony, resolution of a problem
Cowardice, giving up
Beating the competition

Patterns and Correspondences
The Wands = rules the personality, ego, and personal power
Suit of cards = clubs
Timeline = days to weeks
Number 5 = the turning point
Zodiac sign = Leo
Element = Fire

Five of Wands Reading for Love
A tarot card about competition, conflict, and rivalry is never a good sign for love or romance.

If you are looking for a new relationship, you need a radical change. What you've done in the past won't work now. Change your online profile to showcase the real you, work with a relationship coach, join a MeetUp or group exercise class, and totally commit to finding the love you want. Don't settle for anything less.

If you are in a relationship, beware outside influences in competition for your lover's attention (or even your own). Use your competitive spirit to bring the relationship closer together.

Bring the focus back to your partnership by doing "activities" together. Anything physically active and in a group setting will be a great way to deepen your bond. Maybe you could learn a martial art together, then practice at home on top of the mattress? Naked, of course.

FIVE OF WANDS READING FOR WORK
The Five of Wands is about competition, rivalry, and conflict. In the business world, you could be facing intense competition with your company and products, or you could find someone is gunning for your job.

Either way, you'll have to commit to reaching your goals at a level that scares you. This means changing your daily routines, beliefs, and habits quickly so you can work with absolute focus and clarity. There is no more room for daydreams and wishes. You need to Do The Work. There are NO exceptions or excuses.

If you work independently, it could be the struggle is between your limitless creativity and your discipline. Focus and commit to doing the work. Don't get distracted by every new possibility and shiny idea. Your creativity needs to serve your goals, instead of distracting you from them.

If you have been putting full effort into a project, you may see your efforts are futile. Instead of giving up, find a new way. Search for a creative solution with fewer challenges and conflict.

FIVE OF WANDS READING FOR HEALTH
This is a physically active card. If you are looking to increase your general health and fitness, look toward group activities or a competitive team sport. Join a dodgeball league, sign up for a Krav Maga class, or get your friends together for flag football.

If you are struggling with your health, this is not the time to accept the situation or take half measures. You'll have to fight. This means being the squeaky wheel with your doctor and the insurance companies. It is your responsibility to get the time, attention, and answers you need. Rally a strong group of supporters behind you, so you can go into battle prepared.

Use the fighting spirit of this card as inspiration. Commit to your goals and never, ever, ever give up.

FIVE OF WANDS READING FOR MONEY AND FINANCES

Financially, it's time for you to focus and create the discipline to defeat your past bad habits and mistakes. You are fighting for your financial future and every dollar saved is proof of your commitment and determination. You are building your character as much as you are building your net worth.

Don't let the peer pressure of trying to keep up with the Joneses derail you from your own goals. The Joneses are miserably in debt and stay up every night wondering how they're going to pay the light bill. Don't hold yourself to standards you didn't set. Create a set of standards, values, and rules for yourself and then hold yourself accountable to what you have determined is important.

Use the power of a competitive group to create new habits and reach your goals. Find a financial accountability group or join an online community of people who are changing their habits. Use your competitive spirit, instead of being used by it.

FIVE OF WANDS READING FOR SPIRITUAL GUIDANCE

This is not a spiritual card. The Five of Wands is very practical.

If you have been struggling on your spiritual path, find a new and creative solution with less conflict. There are too many obstacles on the path you're currently on. Get off this path and find a new one. But don't give up or pull back. Put in the discipline and effort to see this through.

This card is about committing to what you want. You have to figure out what is worth fighting for in your life. What are your values and commitments? What are non-negotiable? Once you know what you will never compromise on, you can go into battle prepared to win.

And, yes, living your life deeply in line with your personal values and non-negotiable commitments is a spiritual undertaking! You must walk your talk, even when (especially when!) it is difficult and you are challenged.

Six of Wands

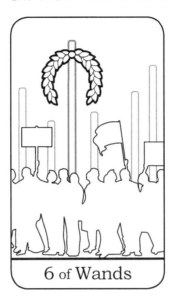

6 of Wands

The Six of Wands is a positive card. Following the challenges and conflict of the Five of Wands, this card represents the victories and recognition you've gained. You have overcome your challenges and are hearing the applause and respect you've earned from your triumph. You are the leader and you are on the right path. This is not time to rest on your laurels, of course. Continue doing the work that brought you to this point. But for a moment you can take a deep breath and celebrate your position. You've earned it.

Traditionally, the Six of Wands looks similar to the Knight court cards. It shows a returning hero with a parade or procession behind him. In the foreground, a man on a horse is holding a wand. At the top of the wand is a wreath of laurel leaves and he has a crown of laurel around his head. The spectators in the background are holding wands, too.

This is a great card for advancement and recognition. People have noticed your efforts and you can expect to be rewarded. It may not be financial recognition, but the rewards will be significant and will improve your position, confidence, and popularity.

Occasionally, this card simply means good news is coming your way.

Keywords for the Six of Wands Tarot Card
Victory, triumph
Popularity, recognition, respect
Confidence
Good news

Keywords for the Six of Wands Reversed
Fall from grace, an epic fail
Abandoning a project or cause
Betrayal
Lack of confidence

Patterns and Correspondences
The Wands = rules the personality, ego, and personal power
Suit of cards = clubs
Timeline = days to weeks
Number 6 = harmony, hearth, and safe harbors
Zodiac sign = Leo
Element = Fire

Six of Wands Reading for Love
The Six of Wands is a card about popularity, recognition, and visibility. You can't hide away anymore. People are looking to you for direction and they are finding you very, very attractive.

Whatever struggles you've faced in the past, you have worked through them. Receive the attention and recognition with grace and confidence. They see something in you that you might not even see in yourself!

If you are looking for new love, you may soon be approached by an ideal partner (or more than one!). You are so popular and enticing people can't help but notice your charms. Keep putting yourself out there and you'll soon receive a message with good news.

If you are in a relationship, you can feel confident in your partnership. You have overcome challenges together and you are on the right path. Continue showing appreciation to your partner and doing the work to bring you even closer together.

Six of Wands Reading for Work

The Six of Wands is a wonderful card, professionally. All of the challenges you've faced are over and you are being recognized for your efforts. This is a great card if you are looking for a promotion, recognition, or an award. All signs point to success!

Put yourself out there by asking for new, challenging projects and nominating or volunteering yourself for opportunities that will enhance your visibility. You will get what you ask for, so ask for exactly what you want. Think big, then think even bigger!

Be sure to thank everyone who has helped you! You didn't get here alone and you will want to celebrate with the people who helped and mentored you along the way.

Six of Wands Reading for Health

If you are looking for news regarding your health, it is likely to come soon and be positive. Until then, keep taking action on what you know works. Push harder on the areas where you have already seen success and double-down on what is working. Focus on your strengths and make them even stronger.

If you are struggling with your health, this card is about finding creative solutions to overcome your challenges. The traditional path won't bring you success.

You will have to make changes to your life, but you will be supported if you involve your friends and family as well as health professionals. Put yourself at the center of team to support you and celebrate every success.

Six of Wands Reading for Money and Finances

Financially, things are improving. This card brings good news about your financial situation. All the hard work is finally paying off.

Continue doing the work and stay committed to your goals. Just because you are seeing rewards and recognition of your hard work doesn't mean you get to slack off. Stay the course and enjoy your success, but don't lose sight of why you are doing this work.

People are watching you and are inspired by what you are doing (even if you don't realize it). Your actions matter and your opportunities are spreading far outside your sphere of influence.

Six of Wands Reading for Spiritual Guidance

The Six of Wands often is a messenger carrying great news. You are gaining insight and confidence on your spiritual journey. While you don't need outside affirmation of your efforts, it is still nice to be recognized.

Accept the praise and accept you enjoy it. There's no shame in being human and having human needs. You are on the right path, so continue what you have been doing.

Use your influence and wisdom to shine a light on the path for others. Reach out to people who seem to be struggling and offer your guidance. You don't have to give advice. Instead, tell them your story and share your experiences, mistakes, and lessons learned.

SEVEN OF WANDS

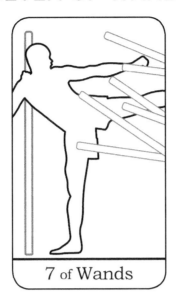

7 of Wands

When you are being tested, the Seven of Wands tarot card tells you to stand your ground. You must defend yourself against the bullies, energy vampires, and "helpful" people who think they know what is best for you. They know nothing. Only you know what is best for you. You must stand up for yourself and defend what is most important to you. Your steadfastness will pay off. Don't compromise or settle for less than what you need and desire.

Traditionally, the Seven of Wands shows a man at the top of a hill, using a wand to defend his position from the six wands attacking below him. You don't see the attackers, but his facial expression indicates this is a serious attack.

This card is about standing your ground when you are challenged. It's about honoring and protecting your goals and values so you can create the life you were meant to live. This card is about power, agency, and control. You won't let yourself be a victim any longer.

You have to go against the crowd and blaze your own defiant path. Do not let anyone stand in your way.

In some cases, this card can have a less intense message about teaching, writing, or self-employment. In professional settings, this card represents competition, owning your skills, and presenting your work proudly to the public.

Keywords for the Seven of Wands Tarot Card
Courage against bullies
Defend what is yours
Competition is stiff
Self-defense, defiance

Keywords for the Seven of Wands Reversed
Surviving a threat
Having weak boundaries
Giving up, quitting

Patterns and Correspondences
The Wands = rules the personality, ego, and personal power
Suit of cards = clubs
Timeline = days to weeks
Number 7 = surety and inner wisdom
Zodiac sign = Leo
Element = Fire

Seven of Wands Reading for Love
If you are looking for love, the competition is fierce. But so are you! Get clear on the type of person you want to be with and the type of relationship you want to have. Once you know what you want, communicate your wishlist clearly to your friends, dates, and potential partners.

Telling the truth is scary and getting specific may feel like you're limiting your options. You are! That's the point. You're unwilling to settle any longer.

So you must tell the truth. Even on a first date. Even if it ruins your chances with your hottie crush. Even though you're scared you'll be alone forever. The Seven of Wands is a card about getting rid of the good and good-enough so you can have something great. Telling the truth is the only way to get what you want.

If you are in a relationship, someone is pressing your boundaries hard. It may be your partner, a family member, or rival. Get clear on what your boundaries are and take action to maintain them. Don't compromise or settle on what is vitally important to you.

SEVEN OF WANDS READING FOR WORK

In this competitive environment, first get clear on your goals and values. Define what are you willing to compromise to reach your goals and what you won't compromise no matter what.

Once you know where your line is, you can defend it. You can trust yourself because you know what matters.

Commit to protecting what is yours. Don't let anyone steal or take credit for your work. Build your resources so you will have a strong defensive stance when you are inevitably attacked. Hire a good lawyer and use a contract every time you purchase or provide a service. Get good insurance. Be proactive about protecting your assets and your work.

If you have critics or haters (and if you're doing anything awesome, you will), celebrate them! Have you ever known a hater who was more successful and committed than you? Of course not! People who are happy, successful, and grateful never tear other people down. There's a reason they want to tear you down to their level. It's because you are so far above them!

If you are looking to become a teacher, start your own business, or write professionally, this card is a good omen. Treat your work seriously and Turn Pro.

SEVEN OF WANDS READING FOR HEALTH

If you are struggling with your health, take charge. Don't let others (not even your doctors) control the situation. They will never care about your body as much as you do.

Get everything in writing and make sure you fully understand what is being said. Ask questions until you understand and write down their answers (or record audio with their permission). Don't be bullied into accepting information because you feel embarrassed, ignorant, scared, or rushed. Scary health situations are stressful so you might not remember what questions to ask or what was said. You need to be your own advocate, so write things down and take as much time as you need.

If you are looking to get back in shape, trust your body. Just because your personal trainer says yoga is the right choice doesn't mean it's the right choice for you. Do the work, but do it your way. If you enjoy competitive activities or team sports, use the energy of competition to drive and motivate yourself to become healthier.

Seven of Wands Reading for Money

Put up good boundaries around your money and protect what you have. Get good insurance and set up extremely strong passwords everywhere online. Open up your bank, credit card, insurance, and investment statements and read through every line. Take control and take responsibility for what is yours. Hire someone to help you and ask questions until you understand every single thing. Get everything in writing and don't trust anyone to manage your money for you. (Hire financial advisers, not money managers). They will never care about your financial situation as much as you do. No matter how much you trust your financial adviser, accountant, or investment club, it is your responsibility to understand what is happening with your money. No one is born knowing what a REIT is. We all have to learn. You may think finances and investing is boring, but when it's your money it gets interesting very quickly!

Seven of Wands Reading for Spiritual Guidance

If you are being challenged about your beliefs, stand your ground. This happens often in traditional religion, but even in enlightened spiritual communities there can be significant peer pressure to do things "the one right way."

You don't have to follow the traditional or common path. You know what your soul is calling for. Trust your intuition before you trust any one else. Walk your own path.

EIGHT OF WANDS

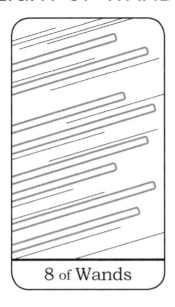

8 of Wands

The Eight of Wands is an unusual card. Traditionally, the card shows eight wands flying through the air without people or a visual representation of the card's story. Despite the simplicity of this card, it's actually easy to read.

The Eight of Wands tarot card is about important news flying through the air toward you. It can also represent something quickly changing in your life.

This is a time for excitement and action, so don't hold back.

If you meet someone new, be prepared for a whirlwind romance. Cupid's arrows are flying!

Whatever your situation, you are in the home stretch. You've done 80% of the work and the results are flying toward you. Keep doing whatever you've been doing and prepare yourself for huge success. Everything you've worked for is coming quickly to fruition.

This is also a great card for travel, especially if you will be flying.

Keywords for the Eight of Wands Tarot Card
Speed, action, rapid change
Air travel
Important news arrives
A whirlwind romance

Keywords for the Eight of Wands Reversed
Delay, frustrations
Traffic jams
Travel plans canceled

Patterns and Correspondences
The Wands = rules the personality, ego, and personal power
Suit of cards = clubs
Timeline = days to weeks
Number 8 = mastery and prosperity
Zodiac sign = Sagittarius
Element = Fire

Eight of Wands Reading for Love
The Eight of Wands is a fantastic card for love and relationships. Things are moving quickly in the direction you desire.

If you are looking for a new relationship, someone is coming into your life to quickly sweep you off your feet. Keep your eyes out for someone who "pops up out of thin air" into your life.

You can't sit at home in a bathrobe waiting for this mysterious stranger to magically appear, though. Put yourself in environments where you will meet the type of partner you desire and don't hold back. This is not the time to play hard-to-get or be coy. Making the first move is strongly encouraged! The harder you work, the faster you will see the results you crave.

If you are currently in a relationship, things are happening rapidly. There will be news or a rapid change in your existing situation. Use the other cards in the spread to see if this new situation will be good or bad. This card alone is a positive omen.

Eight of Wands Reading for Work

Professionally, things are finally coming together. You've put in the hard work and will quickly see results. Keep doing the work, but prepare for a positive change. Build your financial and energetic reserves, maintain your network, and gather a support system.

When the news arrives, you will have to move quickly. The only thing guaranteed is rapid change, so make yourself as prepared as you can be for all possible outcomes.

If you travel for work, this card may indicate another business trip.

Eight of Wands Reading for Health

Things are changing rapidly for you, health-wise. If you've been taking care of yourself, this will be a positive change. If you've let your health slide, be prepared for problems.

No matter what, this is a card for action. You must take charge and do the work. There's no possibility for slacking or procrastination anymore. Everything you've done (or haven't done) will show results soon.

Every step you take toward health will move you quickly toward success. Every step you take away from health will bring you pain and suffering. Every step matters! Don't slack off now.

Even positive change can be challenging, especially when it is rapid. Build your support system if you are feeling discouraged, overwhelmed, or frightened. You don't have to face this challenge alone.

Eight of Wands Reading for Money and Finances

Important news arrives regarding your financial situation. Be prepared for quick changes. You may even need to take rapid action regarding money.

If you've been financially wise, you'll start to see the benefits of compound interest and your investments. Things rapidly improve from here. Keep doing the work and take disciplined action. You are exactly where you want to be.

If you are financially struggling, your situation will quickly make a turn for the worse if you don't make changes now. Do whatever you have to do to set things right. Reach out for help, be radically honest about your situation, and face the truth. Nothing will change for the better until you change your choices and actions. Changing this situation around is 100% within your control.

Eight of Wands Reading for Spiritual Guidance

The Eight of Wands indicates quick change and important news. Spiritually, this card represents the final push you make toward understanding yourself and your role in the world around you.

The knowledge and new ideas are coming to you so rapidly it sometimes feels like you can't keep up. Start recording what you are learning and discovering in a journal. Not only will writing things down help you sort out your ideas, but it will act as a record of your personal growth.

Nine of Wands

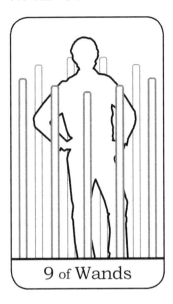

9 of Wands

The Nine of Wands tarot card is the card for courage and persistence in the face of challenges.

Traditionally, this card shows a man tightly gripping a wand, looking off to the side. He looks suspicious and paranoid, and his head is wrapped in a bandage. Eight wands are stuck in the ground behind him, creating a fence or barrier.

When you're feeling defensive and hurt, the Nine of Wands reminds you that you can handle anything if you summon your final reserves and stand for what you believe in.

This card can be a warning to watch your back. Without being paranoid, create strong boundaries and defenses to protect the things you've built.

You have learned many lessons recently. Be sure you actually implement what you've learned by changing your actions (and, if necessary, your words, thoughts, and beliefs). Change is difficult, but necessary. You are definitely strong enough to handle this challenge.

Keywords for the Nine of Wands Tarot Card
Courage, perseverance
Defense, paranoia, boundaries
Lessons learned through experience
Protect what you've built

Keywords for the Nine of Wands Reversed
Isolation ends
Seek reinforcements
Don't be so defensive

Patterns and Correspondences
The Wands = rules the personality, ego, and personal power
Suit of cards = clubs
Timeline = days to weeks
Number 9 = completion, wisdom attained
Zodiac sign = Sagittarius
Element = Fire

Nine of Wands Reading for Love
This is a lonely card. If it shows up in a love reading, take a step back.
Get absolutely clear on the type of relationship you want to have and
the type of person you want to be with.

If you are looking for a new relationship, don't be discouraged by all the
fuckboys and spambots you encounter. There is someone perfect for
you, so don't become one of the embittered and hopeless lonely people
who build their walls so high they never find love. You must support
your search with hope and determination. Take care of yourself as you
look for someone new. Enjoy the process, but also protect your heart.
Don't let yourself fall for the first person who shows you attention or
seems like a perfect match. Take your time and put yourself first.

If you are struggling in your current relationship, make sure you aren't
pushing each other's buttons on purpose. With courage, persistence,
and maybe a bit of therapy, you'll be able to come together again, even
stronger than you were before.

Nine of Wands Reading for Work

As you've experienced, not everyone is a joy to work with. Without getting paranoid or overly defensive, create strong boundaries for how you let other people treat you. Protect the work you do and treat all your output and assets as valuable.

You've learned many lessons through experience and this is the time to put those lessons into practice. You can handle this and more, so summon your courage and perseverance and get to work.

If you are feeling discouraged or disappointed, you are absolutely strong enough to get through this rough patch. This experience will make you stronger and teach you vital lessons you will need in the future.

Nine of Wands Reading for Health

This card can represent a "wounded warrior," which is not a good omen for health. If you have any lingering health issues, seek treatment for them now. This is not something you can put off any longer.

If you are struggling with maintaining good health habits, do not give up or give in to hopelessness. Build up your good health habits day by day, and you will see them pay off. It won't happen as quickly as you'd like, but it will happen.

Make things as easy for yourself as possible by investing in quality tools, supportive friendships, and professional help. You're worth it and those investments will make a difference in your success.

You're so close to the finish line. No matter what obstacles are in your way, you can do this. Don't give up now!

Nine of Wands Reading for Money and Finances

This is not a good card when looking to make investments or big financial risks. Instead, defend and protect what you have.

Get good insurance and read your policies completely. Write an official will. Open all of your financial statements and ask questions until you completely understand what they say. Don't let fear, overwhelm, or your ego get in the way of asking questions until you feel comfortable and confident with your financial situation.

If you are struggling financially, identify the habits and beliefs keeping you from earning, saving, and wisely using your money and your time. You have been learning these financial lessons through the school of hard knocks and it's time to put the lessons into practice. Your financial situation won't change until you make changes in your habits and behavior.

Making mistakes is how we all learn. It is your responsibility to take the lessons and change your behavior so you never make the same mistakes again.

NINE OF WANDS READING FOR SPIRITUAL GUIDANCE
This is a test of faith. Literally.

The Nine of Wands reminds you of your strength in the face of adversity. We all face challenges. Some of those challenges test the very core of who we are.

With courage, persistence, and compassion you will be able to address the obstacles standing in the way of your faith. You can handle anything, even this. Keep walking your path, even though it looks more like a mountain climb. You are building and strengthening your beliefs, values, and faith with every challenge you face and overcome.

TEN OF WANDS

10 of Wands

The Ten of Wands tarot card is the story of modern life. When you are burdened by too many responsibilities and commitments, the Ten of Wands reminds you to shrug off your load and put your own needs first.

Whether you are a carrying the burden for others, or have to delegate and declutter more from your life, you no longer can do it all on your own. You need help.

There is too much stress in your life and too much is landing on your shoulders. Instead of success, all of your hard work is leading toward exhaustion and burnout. You can't go on like this. You must put yourself and your own needs first. Learn to say no. And say it loudly and often.

In the RW-based traditional deck, the Ten of Wands shows a man carrying ten wands. His back is to the viewer and he is hunched over with his burden. It looks like he is walking to the village, which is far in the distance.

Keywords for the Ten of Wands Tarot Card
Too many responsibilities
Carrying the load for others
You're trying to do it all
Put yourself and your needs first

Keywords for the Ten of Wands Reversed
Avoiding responsibility
Finally saying no
Taking a break
Courage and liberation from your burdens

Patterns and Correspondences
The Wands = rules the personality, ego, and personal power
Suit of cards = clubs
Timeline = days to weeks
Number 10 = beginning again with wisdom
Zodiac sign = Sagittarius
Element = Fire

Ten of Wands Reading for Love
This isn't a great card for love. The Ten of Wands is about feeling overburdened by expectations, commitments, and responsibilities. You are being pulled in too many different directions and are losing your center. You don't even remember what you want any more!

If you are looking for a new relationship, the timing isn't right. Finding (and maintaining) a healthy relationship requires commitment, focus, and dedication. You don't have anything to spare right now.

You have too many other things on your plate you have to deal with first. Before you can determine what you want, you must get rid of everything you know isn't a good fit. You'll know when the time is right for love - it will feel easy and relaxed.

If you are in an existing relationship, you are carrying too much of the load yourself. Your partner isn't fully participating. The responsibilities and burdens are all on your shoulders. This isn't fair and it isn't loving, for either of you.

Quit enabling your partner's weaknesses. Quit taking the "easy way" - you're not doing anyone any favors. Start saying "no" and holding to your boundaries and values. Your partner will respect you more and more importantly, you'll start to respect yourself again.

TEN OF WANDS READING FOR WORK
Overwhelm. Stress. Burnout. Exhaustion. Does this sound like your life?

You have been trying to do it all. Instead of seeing the success you expected, all you see is more responsibilities, burdens, obligations and pain.

You need to delegate. This is not negotiable. You need help. And you must ask for it. No one will do this for you.

Get rid of the tasks that aren't in your job description, that you aren't great at, or that you don't enjoy. Learn to set and communicate your boundaries and quit doing the work of others.

While it may seem like more work in the short-term to delegate and train others, it is necessary. You don't have the option to avoid it any longer. You must remove some of the workload or you will damage your company and your career.

TEN OF WANDS READING FOR HEALTH
You absolutely must take care of yourself and put your health first. It seems noble and responsible to make sure your family (and friends and coworkers) are all fed, clothed, entertained, healthy, and happy. But if you focus on their needs, you end up last.

And that is simply unacceptable. If you collapse, what will your friends and family do then?

You can no longer put yourself last. Your health is suffering because of it.

Prioritize your health and put your own oxygen mask on first. Don't try to go this alone. Ask for as much help as you need and then ask for more.

You will not get respect or love by being a martyr. You win no awards by putting other people's needs ahead of yours. If you continue to put yourself last, you will die without anyone (including yourself) knowing who you are. Is that what you want?

Ten of Wands Reading for Money and Finances

Until you are completely debt-free (and this includes your mortgage, the cars, and your student loans), you won't know what freedom actually means. You can no longer ignore the burden of your past mistakes. You must create a plan to get out of debt, stay out of debt, and begin investing in your future.

Declutter your possessions. You have too much stuff weighing you down. Hold a garage sale, put up a post on Ebay, Freecycle, or Craigslist, and get rid of everything you don't use, love, and need. The extra money will help create your financial future and the extra space around the house will give you less to clean and maintain.

Simplify your activities and routines. Pare everything down so you have fewer decisions to make. When you simply everything down to what you truly value, you'll see how little you need to be happy and content.

Ten of Wands Reading for Spiritual Guidance

The Ten of Wands is about feeling oppressed by your decisions and responsibilities. Spiritually, too many of your past beliefs are no longer true, yet you're carrying them around as if they are written in stone. Examine each of your beliefs and shrug off the beliefs that no longer suit you. Become extremely intentional in what you do, say, and own.

Service toward others can become a burden. Although charity and good works are commonly associated with a spiritual path, they can become a drag if done in excess or for the wrong reasons. Examine what you value and eliminate everything that isn't in alignment with who you are, what you believe, and what you want for your life.

PAGE OF WANDS

Page of Wands

In the traditional RW-based deck, the Page of Wands tarot card shows a young man delicately gripping his wand. Caressing it. Stroking it. Looking adoringly at his rod.

What??!? It really does.

Despite the rather phallic nature of this card, it doesn't have much to do with love, lust, or babies.

Instead, this card usually represents a fiery, active, creative young person in your life. This is likely to be someone enthusiastic, loyal, rebellious and full of life.

More generally, it can also represent a student, a foreigner, or a stranger.

If not an actual person, this card can also mean a new creative project, adventure, or idea. It could represent a new career path or course of study. There is encouraging and exciting news, possibly from an unexpected source. This is the spark of a new idea or attraction. It will lead you someplace very interesting!

Keywords for the Page of Wands Tarot Card
A student or rebel
The spark of a new idea or project
Exciting news from an unexpected source
Adventure or travel

Keywords for the Page of Wands Reversed
Delay or disappointment
Dishonesty
Apathy, a slacker
Immaturity

Patterns and Correspondences
The Wands = rules the personality, ego, and personal power
Suit of cards = clubs
Timeline = days to weeks
The Page = info and messages to grow new understanding
Element = Fire

Page of Wands Reading for Love
Cupid is back! This card often represents the spark of a new love or attraction. Be open to new people who enter your life and keep your eyes out for a creative rebel or foreigner who will take you on a new adventure.

If you are in an existing relationship, the spark comes back. Together you get great news and begin working on a fun idea or project. This brings you closer together. You can't sit around waiting for change to happen, though. You must seize every opportunity and keep your eyes out for fun, new activities you and your partner can do together.

This card can indicate travel and adventure, so if you are looking to spice up your love life, consider taking a trip far outside of your ordinary routine.

Page of Wands Reading for Work

The Page of Wands often indicates a new career path or course of study. If you are looking for a sign, this is it! This new direction will lead you on an adventure of creativity and inspiration.

You may get unexpected and positive news from a child, stranger, or someone outside your normal sphere. Listen to this person! The message they bring is unusual, but encouraging.

New projects, ideas, passions, and creative adventures are all positive. Follow your spark and keep an open mind about where it leads you. You are at the beginnings of a new adventure. It will (eventually) require a lot of work, faith, and commitment, but for right now, it's all fun, joy, and play. Follow the threads of what you love and keep moving toward the activities you enjoy. Your heart knows where you belong.

Page of Wands Reading for Health

If you are trying to get healthy, look to the children and young people in your life. Model your activity on theirs and have fun. Lots and lots of fun. Spend as much time with them as you can, playing at their level. Exaggerate your interests and joy until your enthusiasm is a beacon for others.

There has been too much dull drudgery in your life lately. You have to find your spark again. The good news is your spark is waiting for you to light the fire. If an idea or activity seems interesting or fun, spend time playing with it. Learn and share what you are doing. Be enthusiastic and you will draw in others who can help your health and fitness goals.

For more serious health issues, keep your eyes and ears open for encouraging news from an unexpected source. Someone may have a message for you to help you look at your problems from a new perspective.

Page of Wands Reading for Money and Finances

You may get some strange and exciting news from an unusual source. Don't jump on any hot stock tips or investments without doing your research, but keep an open mind. Just because some young punk kid with facial piercings and a devil tattoo carries the message doesn't mean you shouldn't listen to it.

Both information and encouragement will shortly become present in your life. Release your fears about money and your past mistakes. Look toward the future and take action to fund your dreams.

Starting a new project or following a new interest doesn't necessarily cost a lot of money, so don't let that excuse hold you back. Brainstorm at least 10 different ways you can accomplish your goal or investigate a new idea without using money. Use your creativity in funding the project, not only in accomplishing it.

You may be starting a new course of study or career. This requires courage, creativity, enthusiasm…and money. Begin stockpiling your resources now so you have the flexibility to make the change when it comes.

Page of Wands Reading for Spiritual Guidance

Spiritually, a young person or stranger may have a message for you. This inspired new idea will radically alter your view of the world, but it comes from an unusual and unexpected source.

Trust your curiosity. Use your creativity to blow past your usual excuses. The world is much more interesting, flexible, and open than you've been assuming.

Anything and everything is possible. You just have to believe it could happen. Knowing how isn't your job. It's your job to feed the possibilities with faith and enthusiasm. Let the Universe do the rest.

You may begin walking a completely new and unexpected spiritual path. This is exciting! Release your fears and keep an open mind to everything you encounter.

KNIGHT OF WANDS

Knight of Wands

In the traditional RW-deck, the Knight of Wands tarot card shows a rather feminine-looking knight charging into battle. This card feels less violent than the Knight of Swords, but it is just as forward-moving and active.

This card, like all the court cards, can represent someone in your life, a role you play, or a message you are ready to hear.

If this is an actual person in your life, the Knight of Wands will represent a person (male or female) who is lusty, passionate, and free-spirited.

Despite this crusader's free-spirit, this is not someone who is playful or carefree. The Knight of Wands has got a sense of purpose and a very strong will.

This person thrives on the challenge of discovering new projects and ideas. They always follow the path least traveled. This is someone who loves adventure and appears fearless, sexy and brave.

When it comes to your own life, this knight is committed to helping you grow through the creative process. They want you to pursue your own dreams with enthusiasm. The Knight of Wands will help you get your projects started and keep you encouraged and committed during the journey.

Whatever the question is, the Knight's answer is: You have the energy and skills you need, so go for it!

In a practical sense, this card can also indicate a journey, changes in the home, or relocating to a new place.

Keywords for the Knight of Wands Tarot Card
Passion, motivation, desire
Adventure, relocation, a journey
A charismatic and daring person
Go for it!

Keywords for the Knight of Wands Reversed
Chaotic and mis-directed energy
Lots of heart, but no follow through
A person who cheats
Erectile dysfunction

Patterns and Correspondences
The Wands = rules the personality, ego, and personal power
Suit of cards = clubs
Timeline = days to weeks
The Knight = learning and testing new wisdom
Element = Fire

Knight of Wands Reading for Love
The Knight of Wands is sex on a stick. If you are looking for new love, this card is an extremely good omen. Keep your eyes out for a lusty, passionate, aggressive and supportive new partner.

If you are in an existing relationship, beware charismatic and sexy new people who enter your life. It's easy to get distracted by a new lusty adventure when you are bored at home.

Instead of leaping into something new, channel the energy of this card to benefit your current partnership by spicing up activities in the bedroom, both in quality and in quantity. Turn yourself into the Knight of Wands by being honest, brave, and creative in how you ask for what you need from your partner.

Knight of Wands Reading for Work

Any new project or idea is likely to be a great one. If you've been planning, researching, and thinking about something, now is the time to take action on it. No more maybes. This is definitely it!

Of course, this card can also represent an actual person you work with. If so, they likely will serve as a role model or will bring you a message you are ready to hear. This person will be forward-thinking, creative, and enthusiastic.

Occasionally, the Knight of Wands can move too quickly and make mistakes due to haste and daring. Don't let that hold you back, but be prepared. The changes you are making are big and it may take time for others to catch up with your vision.

Knight of Wands Reading for Health

If you are looking to get healthier, partner up with someone who has the qualities of the Knight of Wands. They will make the perfect accountability buddy for you.

Do not hold back. Any action you take will be positive. Consider pairing activity with travel or adventure, like signing up for a half-marathon in another country. Not only will you challenge yourself physically, but you'll be so excited about the trip you won't mind training for the race!

Keep moving forward toward your goals, monitor the results, and correct your course along the way. Don't wait for everything to be perfect before you act.

For more serious health problems, take immediate action. You know what to do (even if you don't want to do it). The Knight of Wands indicates you must move forward in a bold way. Keep at it until you get the answers you need and see the results you want.

KNIGHT OF WANDS READING FOR MONEY

You may receive some financial information from someone who has a bold new idea. The idea looks good, but do your own research before you invest or commit too heavily. The Knight of Wands sometimes risks too much or acts too hastily, so protect yourself before you blindly trust the advice you receive.

If you are struggling financially, this card is a huge wake-up call. You are beyond ready to change your life. You know at your core that you can't continue this way. You must change.

It's painful, but you have finally realized you have been the cause of everything that's currently happening to you (good and bad) and you now see where you have been making excuses and playing the victim. And you're not willing to accept your own bullshit any longer.

The Knight of Wands will lead you through this discovery. You have the will, energy, and direction you need to get started on changing your life. It starts today and you are ready.

KNIGHT OF WANDS READING FOR SPIRITUAL GUIDANCE

Inspiration and creativity are flowing through you. As soon as you come up with a new idea, three others follow right behind it.

But this isn't a card for ideas and inspiration. It's about action.

You are ready to commit to your spiritual goals. Whatever that means to you, you have the motivation and passion necessary to see this through. You're ready.

This card often indicates a real person in your life. Look at your extended social circle for someone with an inspiring message about your spiritual path. Listen with an open heart and an open mind to this person, even if it seems to come from an unusual source.

QUEEN OF WANDS

Queen of Wands

The Queen of Wands tarot card shows a woman sitting on a throne, holding a wand in one hand and a sunflower in the other. There is a black cat in front of her.

This Queen is self-assured with lots of personal magnetism. She has explored and mastered the dark places of her soul (often shown as a black cat) and has come out transformed.

This card can represent an actual person in your life, a role you must play, or a message you need to hear.

If this card is representing someone in your life, it will be someone (male or female) who is assertive and popular, with overflowing confidence.

Professionally, the Queen will be in an executive position, probably the boss. In the home realm, this is someone who is a gracious and easy host, with a deep love for animals. Despite her comfort and ease, she's more of a lioness than a house cat.

This Queen has achieved self-knowledge and self-mastery. She easily balances a boundless creative energy with such radiant self-assurance that you can't help but be drawn in by her enthusiasm and commitment.

She's ambitious and powerful, but she doesn't hog the spotlight. When this card represents a role you must play or a message you are ready to hear, the Queen of Wands wants you to go for your own dreams and will help you commit big-time to your passion and desires.

KEYWORDS FOR THE QUEEN OF WANDS TAROT CARD
An assertive and passionate person
Intense courage and self-assurance
A master of self-knowledge and self-transformation
Boundless creative energy

KEYWORDS FOR THE QUEEN OF WANDS REVERSED
An aggressive and demanding person
A wallflower or shrinking violet
Dying passion, no real fire

PATTERNS AND CORRESPONDENCES
The Wands = rules the personality, ego, and personal power
Suit of cards = clubs
Timeline = days to weeks
The Queen = inner wisdom and mastery
Element = Fire

QUEEN OF WANDS READING FOR LOVE
If you are looking for a new partner, keep your eyes out for a confident and creative person to enter your life. She (or he) is hot-hot-hot!

And if you're in an existing relationship, you can use this queen's fire to bring some spark back into your partnership. The bedroom is a great place to begin, but it's only the starting point.

The Queen of Wands wants you to know yourself deeply. She wants you to become the most you version of yourself, so you can share everything (even the shameful and scary bits) with your partner. To truly have a real partnership - one for the ages - you must be open, vulnerable, and courageous. But she knows you can do it!

Queen of Wands Reading for Work

This card likely represents an ambitious, assertive, and magnetic woman in your professional life. She's the perfect mentor or guide.

If there's no one who fits that description, use the message of this card and model your actions on the queen's. She wants you to dig deep to get to the core of your desires and then take a big risk to bring them to fruition.

You are ready to commit with complete dedication and focus. Only with full commitment will you begin to know and understand yourself. This commitment to your dreams will result in a spontaneous and intense transformation that leaves you self-assured, confident, and fully alive. Go for it!

Queen of Wands Reading for Health

The Queen of Wands has the energetic creativity of a child. She's powered from within and doesn't let the muggles get her down.

This card may represent an active and popular person in your life. If so, she or he has a message for you and will make an excellent role model or guide relating to your health.

If you are facing bigger health problems, explore your fears and secrets. There's something deeper here not being addressed. Balance your logical mind with your intuition to find new answers.

Queen of Wands Reading for Money

This card is a positive omen for money and finances, if you are willing to do the work. This queen loves her king - but she doesn't need him. She's already rescued herself. You must do the same.

If you are looking for advice, find the most ambitious and successful person you know. They will have a message for you and will be able to guide you toward your goals.

You can model your financial behavior on this queen. She's gone deep within to confront her darkest secrets and has accepted all her past mistakes. There is no shame in being human, but if you see behavior that needs to change, you are the only one who can change it.

Queen of Wands Reading for Spiritual Guidance

If this card is representing an actual person in your life, they will likely have a spiritual message or question for you. If there is no one who fits the description of this queen, you may want to embody her qualities yourself.

The Queen of Wands took a trip through hell to get where she is today. She's had to fight for her knowledge, self-assurance, and success. Although your spiritual questions won't be easily answered, they will be resolved as long as you don't give up the quest.

And once they are, whoa! Your transformation will be incredible.

KING OF WANDS

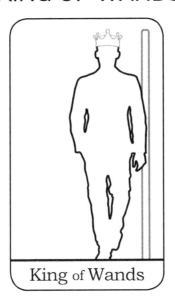

King of Wands

The King of Wands tarot card brings together all of the lessons of the Wands suit. He's a wise leader, charismatic authority figure, and inspired creator.

Traditionally, the King of Wands card shows a man in profile, sitting on a throne. He is holding a wand and wearing a crown, and there are salamanders decorating his throne.

This feels like a solid and steady card, especially compared to the passion and heat of the other Wands court cards. Don't be deceived. This King's got swagger and knows when to use it.

Like all court cards, this card can represent an actual person in your life, a role you need to play, or a message you are ready to hear. If it's a real person, it will be an alpha leader, perhaps your boss or another authority figure, who is macho to the core.

This is someone (male or female) who radiates power. The Kind of Wands represents a self-starter with charisma, kindness, and creativity. This person will be intense, powerful, and intimidating.

This King commands you to see your own power. He is the master of his own life and knows everything happening to him has been caused by his thoughts, words, and actions. Everything. He wants you to learn the same.

The King of Wands is an authority at removing obstacles, telling the truth (even when it hurts), and bringing outrageous visions to life. You can bring those qualities into your own life by breaking old patterns and behaviors and by giving up any victim-thinking once and for all.

KEYWORDS FOR THE KING OF WANDS TAROT CARD
An entrepreneur, executive, or self-starter
Swagger, charm, and bold leadership
A master of bold, new ideas
Optimism, power, creativity

KEYWORDS FOR THE KING OF WANDS REVERSED
A bully or dictator
A sexist jerk or cheater
A weakling, or someone with no impact or vision
Erectile dysfunction

PATTERNS AND CORRESPONDENCES
The Wands = rules the personality, ego, and personal power
Suit of cards = clubs
Timeline = days to weeks
The King = expanding and sharing wisdom
Element = Fire

KING OF WANDS READING FOR LOVE
If you are looking for a new romance, keep your eyes open for a charismatic and charming person. If he's male, he'll be a man's man - macho and confident in his masculinity. It it's a woman, she'll be confident and fierce.

When this king comes into your life, be prepared to be overwhelmed. He (or she) may appear restrained on the outside, but he runs deep. This guy is full of passion, creativity, and power.

If you are in a relationship, use this card to guide your own actions. How can you break your old patterns and beliefs so you no longer have the same struggles and expectations? It's up to you to remove the obstacles standing between you and happiness. No one will do it for you. It's not your partner's job to make you happy.

KING OF WANDS READING FOR WORK

This card likely represents your boss or another professional authority figure. He (or she) might be a mentor, guide, or partner. If so, he's going to swagger with power, confidence, and vision. This isn't bluster, though. He's the real deal.

Professionally, you must learn from this king. Create a bigger vision than you've previously dreamed and then dream even bigger. Once you've got an inspired and meaningful ideal, you can begin working toward it. You must be confident, bold, and creative, so work on building those skills through action and execution.

KING OF WANDS READING FOR HEALTH

The King of Wands is an active and healthy card. If there is someone with this king's qualities in your life, search them out and ask them for help. They will have a message and inspiration for you.

If you are struggling with your health, you could do worse than modeling your thoughts, actions, and beliefs on this king. It will take big and bold change, but you are ready to take control. No more waiting, wishing, or deferring to the experts. You must throw everything at your problems to get them solved.

King of Wands Reading for Money and Finances
This king is an excellent role model for strong financial habits. Find a successful mentor who can guide you to success and then take action on their advice.

You are ready to make big changes, but you have the strength and vision to see this through. There will be challenges, but breaking your old patterns and habits is actually going to be the easy part. Things really get wild once you realize you have 100% of the power to create your own future and anything is possible.

King of Wands Reading for Spiritual Guidance

The King of Wands is an inspiration for spiritual growth. This king is a master of inspired vision and he truly sees deeper than most of us.

He is perceptive and insightful. When he's around, all obstacles seem to disappear, because he makes them disappear by changing his beliefs. It isn't magic. It's his spiritual truth.

Everything he believes comes true. And he is the cause of everything that happens in his life.

Find someone who represents the King of Wands and ask them for guidance and advice. You'll be surprised by how caring, thoughtful, and compassionate this king can be.

THANK YOU!

Thanks for reading and using this book. I hope you've found it useful. **If this book has been helpful, please leave a review at the site you bought it.** Reviews are so important, both for other tarot lovers and to give support to the author. Any feedback is appreciated!

GET MORE FROM THE SIMPLE TAROT

Visit www.TheSimpleTarot.com to get your free, PDF printable Tarot Cheat Sheet.

You'll also find daily tarot prompts, useful tarot spreads, and The Simple Tarot Deck to help make learning (and reading) tarot simple, easy, and fun.

THE SIMPLE TAROT
CHEAT SHEET
with keywords for any RW-based tarot deck

	CUPS water - emotional	PENTACLES earth - physical	SWORDS air - intellect	WANDS fire - creativity
ACE	new baby or relationship, proposal, marriage	new job, raise, promotion, investment, new income	new ideas, new conflict, surgery, mental clarity	new project, inspiration, the urge to create
TWO	romantic love, partnership, proposal, marriage	two choices, multi-tasking, weighing many options	time to compromise or make a decision	waiting for results, make a choice, travel plans
THREE	friendship, celebrations, a circle of support	teamwork, collaboration, skill, quality, craftsmanship	heartbreak, divorce, loss, depression, surgery	teamwork, commerce, expansion, travel
FOUR	apathy, feeling unfulfilled, surprise gifts	greed or desire for long-term security	retreat, rest, renewal, solitude, recovery	homecoming, celebrations, family, friends, reunions
FIVE	loss, regret, grief, feeling abandoned or unloved	poverty, ill health, worry, isolation, financial loss	bullies, theft, violence, abusive relationships	rivalry, challenges, obstacles, sport
SIX	nostalgia, gifts, innocence, reunions	giving or receiving help, generosity	a necessary transition, relocating, moving	victory, award, recognition, good news, success
SEVEN	too many choices, commitment issues	patience, hard work, delayed success, waiting	theft, betrayal, dishonesty, running away	self-defense, protect against competition
EIGHT	withdrawl, retreat, moving on, abandonment	mastering your craft, enjoying your employment	self-imposed restrictions, isolation, imprisonment	speed, action, quick changes, news arrives
NINE	wishes come true, material abundance, good health	luxury, self-sufficience, financial gain, solo pleasures	nightmares, anxiety, grief, depression	keeping & maintaining boundaries, persistance
TEN	family contentment, total love and support	leaving a legacy, retirement, inheritance	complete and painful ending, rock bottom	stress, exhaustion, too many burdens
PAGE	a studious kid, new love, volunteer work	a patient kid, a new job or raise, money news	a curious kid, gossip, spies, prying eyes, truth	an active kid, a new project or creative idea
KNIGHT	a "Prince/ss Charming," romance, proposals	a reliable person, patience, hard work	a fast-talking person, lifestyle change	a lusty and free-spirited person, creativity
QUEEN	a nurturing person, healing, support	a resourceful person, fertility, domesticity	a self-sufficient person, total honesty	a feisty person, confidence, self-assurance
KING	a supportive leader, tolerance, empathy	a solid and practical leader, wise investor	an intentional leader, strategic thought	a bold leader, power, charm, courage

0 - THE FOOL fresh hope, take chances, new paths and adventures, beginnings	**1 - THE MAGICIAN** focused creativity, turning visions into reality, inspired action
2 - THE HIGH PRIESTESS secrets, mystery, intuition, trust yourself	**3 - THE EMPRESS** fertility, creation, pregnancy, abundance, good parenting
4 - THE EMPEROR respect, leadership, strategic planning, a father figure	**5 - THE HIEROPHANT** traditions, conventional expectations, conformity
6 - THE LOVERS partnership, deep love, a choice, the strength of two together	**7 - THE CHARIOT** action and change, a journey, a new vehicle, vroom-vroom
8 - STRENGTH self-love, unconditional love, self-respect, courage	**9 - THE HERMIT** go within for clarity, a quest for personal truth, spiritual illumination
10 - THE WHEEL OF FORTUNE good fortune, a turning point, gambling, luck	**11 - JUSTICE** cause and effect, win-win solutions, the truth comes out
12 - THE HANGED MAN wisdom, self-sacrifice, get a different perspective	**13 - DEATH** big changes, endings, time to move on, rebirth, transformation
14 - TEMPERANCE balance, harmony, patience, self-control, moderation	**15 - THE DEVIL** addiction, greed, envy, materialism, obsession, sexual lust
16 - THE TOWER unwanted change, ruin, disgrace, upheaval, violence	**17 - THE STAR** renewal, hope, inner clarity, miracles, have faith, being in the spotlight
18 - THE MOON unseen problems, voluntary changes, trust your intuition	**19 - THE SUN** material happiness, a joyous outcome, success
20 - JUDGMENT clarity, a final decision, a wake-up call, your life's purpose	**21 - THE WORLD** completing a goal or lesson, emigration, travel, completion

THE SIMPLE TAROT
© 2018 The Simple Tarot

Milton Keynes UK
Ingram Content Group UK Ltd.
UKHW051313151023
430649UK00016B/186